Lucas Aufenkamp

the WIND Principle

Tracking the Movement of God's Spirit
In the Life of a Believer

Destination
Resources

The Wind Principle
Copyright © 2016 by Lucas Aufenkamp

Published by Destination Resources
735 4th St NW
Valley City, ND 58072
www.lucasaufenkamp.com

First Edition

ISBN-13: 978-0692610220
ISBN-10: 0692610227

Cover illustration: Ozerina Anna/Shutterstock
Author Photo: Gemar Photography, Minot, North Dakota

Lucas Aufenkamp has written a wonderful inspirational book in which he weaves the story of David and other Biblical personalities like Joseph and Abraham to illustrate how God moves each of us along a life journey that starts rather unimpressively. From that starting point frequently we find our life route unpredictable, but all the while God is leading us to an unexpected destination. I've certainly found that true in my own life, as has every believer. This is a book which will encourage you in your own life journey – especially in those moments when we experience a sharp turn that we had not foreseen.

DR. GEORGE O. WOOD
General Superintendent of the Assemblies of God

From the first line to the last, *The Wind Principle* captures your attention and holds it while unlocking a key that just might be a life changer.

DANIEL JOHNSON SR.
Author of *Come Home America* and *When You Ask Why*

Lucas Aufenkamp defines *The Wind Principle* as "the process by which God moves a follower of Jesus from the place of simple beginning to the place of His great calling." While not every believer will attain to the calling or prominence of King David, we can all find our rightful place in Christ's Body, the Church. This book is loaded with insights into how the Spirit of God works in and through the life of a believer completely yielded to finding and fulfilling their true calling in Christ. The lasting value of this book will not be gained through a quick read but rather through meditation and study and then allowing the Spirit of God to lead as He wills.

DAVID RAVENHILL
Author & Teacher
Siloam Springs, Arkansas

Pastor Lucas Aufenkamp inspires us to look beyond our present location's limitations to see God's great future plan. *The Wind Principle* challenges us to stay in the process of constant growth—no matter how discouraged we may get along the way. Small beginnings can indeed lead to maximum impact!

> **TIM ENLOE**
> Author/Conference Speaker
> Enloe Ministries/Holy Spirit Conferences
> Wichita, KS

As we experience joy, sorrow and unexpected outcomes—life has a way of clouding our view of our abilities and of God. We easily become dependent on searching for answers we can explain or justify instead of trusting God to direct our steps. The Wind Principle walks through biblical examples and offers practical applications to help us discover how to let go of our preconceived notions and trust the Spirit of God, as well as His plans for our lives.

> **PEBBLES THOMPSON**
> Co-founder of Project Ignite Light
> Rogers, ND

To my parents, Leroy and Bev Aufenkamp.
Thank you for your perseverance and for guiding me into a love of the
Bible and the Church.

CONTENTS

~~~~~

www.thewindprinciple.com

Section 1: An Unimpressive Beginning

Jerusalem, circa 998 B.C.

EVERYONE in the great dining hall came to attention as King David rose from his designated place at the table and retreated toward an interior stairway within the royal residence. The sun was beginning to set over the City of David as the king emerged from the stairwell to the roof of the palace, as he did so often after the evening meal.

It had been an exciting couple days for the king, to say the least. The previous evening David had met with the prophet Nathan, describing his plans for the construction of a grand temple which would serve as the center of Jewish worship. The prophet had given his coveted blessing.

Now David looked from his palace toward the northeast. As he did, he could see a cloud of wheat chaff disperse in the wind from the threshing floor of Araunah the Jebusite. David could envision this location as the ideal site for the temple. It was on that pinnacle that Abraham, centuries earlier, had prepared to offer his son Isaac as a sacrifice in obedience to God. Abraham was stopped moments before driving the knife into his son when God Himself provided a sacrifice in the place of Isaac. Abraham had named this location, "Jehovah Jireh" meaning, *In the Mount of the Lord it shall be provided.* David hoped that one day the site would once again be the place where sacrifices would be provided, this time for the sins of the people.

As David turned his back on the future Temple Mount, emotion rose within him as he looked toward the southwest in the direction of Bethlehem. He could envision now the scene as the shepherds would be preparing to bed down for the night with their flocks, ever aware of the danger that lie just out of view. It had been in those very hills that David had spent countless nights with his father's sheep.

A wave of nostalgia rose within the king as he considered the route that had taken him from the sheepfold to the throne. In that moment he could envision the panorama of his life. The day the prophet Samuel had visited Bethlehem so many years prior was no different than any other. And yet by the end of that day everything had changed.

David was nearly overcome by the satisfaction of the moment as he wondered to himself how he, a simple shepherd, had come so far. One thing the king knew for certain, the process that had brought him to where he was presently was one that was beyond him.

As he thought on the route from the sheepfold to the throne, the king realized that in many ways, not much had changed. Truth be told, he was still a shepherd. As king, the border which surrounded Israel was like the fence which encircled a sheep pen.

There were also the boundaries of right and wrong which he had sought to instill in his people to protect them from danger.

As a young man he had always been willing to stand between the sheep and danger. He recalled two separate occasions when he dealt with a lion and a bear, both of which had attempted to grab one of his father's sheep. "That is why I have chosen you," Jesse would remind David after his youngest son would retell one of those harrowing episodes.

David had witnessed far too many instances when a hired man would flee at the first sign of danger. The chaos that ensued always made him feel sick. He would think to himself, "I'm no hireling," when someone would ask why he would risk his life for his father's sheep.

As king, he was determined that his people would never know the chaos that resulted from the lack of a shepherd. He intended to always be a good shepherd.

The king's thoughts were disrupted as one of his palace guards emerged from the stairwell and bowed slightly before the king. "Excuse me, my king," said the guard. "The prophet Nathan has returned and requests some time." David settled into one of the seats built into the palace wall that rose a few cubits above the roof and answered, "Bring him to me."

The king was not quite sure what to make of Nathan. That he was cut from the same cloth as Samuel, the king's mentor, was without question. David knew also that Nathan heard from God. But there was something about the prophet that always left him just a bit on edge. He loved the word of God that the prophet would bring, but he always knew that there was the potential for uncomfortable correction.

This was the unique position of a Jewish king. Legally he had authority over the prophet. As king he could do whatever he wished. But spiritually, he knew that he needed to submit to Nathan. The prophet was God's mouthpiece. To have the favor of God, David knew he needed to listen to, and obey, the prophet's instruction.

David could hear the "clop, clop" of Nathan's staff as he climbed the stairs. As the prophet emerged from the stairwell, David wondered what would warrant a second visit. As was often the case, the prophet showed little sign of reverence to the king as he approached and began to speak.

The central message of the prophet hit squarely at David's ambitious dream of building a temple to the Lord. Nathan revealed that it would not be David who would construct the temple. That privilege and responsibility would rest on one of his sons who would ascend to the throne after David was gone.

It is within Nathan's message to David that we find the key to the track of his life. In 2 Samuel 7:8-9 we read these words from the prophet to the king:

> "Thus says the Lord of hosts: 'I took you from the sheepfold, from following the sheep to be ruler over My people, over Israel. And I have been with you wherever you have gone, and have cut off all your enemies from before you, and have made you a great name, like the name of the great men who are on the earth.'"

The message was clear. David certainly had a part in the process that brought him to where he currently stood. When facing Goliath he had responded with faith rather than fear. When he had the opportunity to kill Saul, he had chosen to submit to the timing of God, rather than attempting to create his own timing.

These were critical decisions that kept him on the track of the divine plan. But without question, David would not have gone from the sheepfold to the throne without God. It had been the Lord who had brought him to his current position as the king of Israel.

A Long Shot

IN the life of David we find a prime example of the wind principle. It is the process by which God moves a man or woman of God from the place of simple beginnings to the place of His great calling. David's simple beginning was in the sheepfold. It was the type of place that one may have described as a dead-end job. His great calling was that of King of Israel. We find the wind principle described in the third chapter of the Gospel of John.

> "There was a man of the Pharisees named Nicodemus, a ruler of the Jews. This man came to Jesus by night and said to Him, 'Rabbi, we know that You are a teacher come from God; for no one can do these signs that You do unless God is with him.' Jesus answered and said to him, 'Most assuredly, I say to you, unless one is born again, he cannot see the kingdom of God.'
>
> "Nicodemus said to Him, 'How can a man be born when he is old? Can he enter a second time into his mother's

womb and be born?' Jesus answered, 'Most assuredly, I say to you, unless one is born of water and the Spirit, he cannot enter the kingdom of God. That which is born of the flesh is flesh, and that which is born of the Spirit is spirit. Do not marvel that I said to you, "You must be born again." The wind blows where it wishes, and you hear the sound of it, but cannot tell where it comes from and where it goes. So is everyone who is born of the Spirit'" (John 3:1-8).

It is in this last verse that the wind principle is spelled out. "The wind blows where it wishes, and you hear the sound of it, but cannot tell where it comes from and where it goes. So is everyone who is born of the Spirit." This principle reveals the way God works to move us from an insignificant starting point along an unpredictable path to an unexpected destination.

Let's give closer attention to the biblical usage of the word "wind" for a moment.

In the Old Testament we find that the word comes from the Hebrew word *ruach* and is alternately translated as "spirit." In Genesis 1:2 it was the *Ruach* of God that "was hovering over the waters." In Exodus 10:13 it was the *ruach* that blew all night on the Red Sea to create a pathway for Israel.

In Ezekiel 37, we find the prophet taken by God's Spirit into a valley filled with lifeless bones. God instructs Ezekiel to prophesy to the wind, that life and breath would enter the lifeless figures. When the prophet did as instructed, it was to the *ruach* that he prophesied.

Jesus certainly had these usages in mind as He spoke to Nicodemus. What is this *wind* that moves God's people? It is the Holy Spirit.

As we look elsewhere in Scripture, we can gain further understanding about the concept of the wind. In Proverbs 27:16, Solomon notes the futility of trying to restrain the wind. Translate that to our context, and consider the possibilities. When the Wind of God, the Holy Spirit, has begun to move upon your life, there is no outside force that can restrain Him.

In Ecclesiastes 2:11 Solomon speaks of attempting to chase the wind. Skill and charisma can carry a person only so far. At some point their energy comes to an end. But the wind never grows tired. You will go much further toward a meaningful destination in life being moved by God's Spirit than you ever will be able to go carrying yourself.

We are repeatedly surprised at those God calls, though by this time perhaps we should not be. In 1 Corinthians 1:26-27 we read of those God often calls:

> "Not many wise according to the flesh, not many mighty, not many noble, are called. But God has chosen the foolish things of the world to put to shame the wise, and God has chosen the weak things of the world to put to shame the things which are mighty."

Into which category do you fall? Would you be considered foolish or wise by the standards of the world? Judging by this passage, you are more likely to be called by God to something great if you fall in the category of foolish in the world's estimation.

As we look through the Bible we find very few who were qualified for the position to which they were called. They were shepherds, fugitives, and fishermen. Their point of origin certainly did not qualify them to the call of completing a great task. And yet we find them leading a kingdom into its age of glory, delivering a nation from bitter oppression and turning the world upside-down with the message of Jesus.

What is the calling God has on your life? The specifics are impossible to know at the outset. The wind principle reveals that it is impossible to predict the direction in which God's Spirit will move a person. The good news is that God's destination for you will be in line with the goodness of His character. To reach that destination, you are responsible to remain in a position where you can be moved by the Spirit.

God's activity in the life of David is a model for his activity in your life and mine. In the model found in 2 Samuel 7:8-9, we find that God was the One who took David from watching the sheep to ruling over Israel. Along the way God remained with David, removing his enemies and making his name great.

As we progress in the plan of God, there will be seasons which may seem very similar to the years David spent running and hiding from Saul. During these seasons we may be tempted to meddle in the process (see Abraham and Hagar). It is then that God wants us to remember that He will not leave us.

There is always opposition along the route, as there were for David. In this we learn an important lesson. Though Saul was trying to kill him, David never viewed him as the enemy. In Ephesians 6:12, Paul said, "We do not wrestle against flesh and blood, but against...the rulers of the darkness of this age." Although Saul represented an apparent obstacle to the destination and had declared his own little war on David, he always remained submitted to the authority which was over him. In doing so he continued to remain in right relationship with God. There may, at times, be people who seem to stand in the way of the route ahead.

In those cases, take a lesson from David and commit the process to God.

Finally, of David, we read that the Lord made for him "a great name." There would need to come a time when David would need to be known as something more than simply a shepherd. As we look at the life of David, we notice that he never did succumb to the temptation to seek self-advancement. Rather, he was simply faithful when opportunity came.

Resist the urge to try and make a name for yourself. Peter tells us that if we will humble ourselves, God will exalt us "in due time" (1 Peter 5:6). Due time refers to the right time. If you set out to make a name for yourself, you might just succeed, but lack the character to sustain what you have achieved. Surrender your ambition to God and seek to be moved by His Spirit.

The Greatest Glory

Back in my hometown I was known as one who played basketball "above the rim." In reality there were only two or three who knew me that way. In a good-natured way they would joke that I played at a level far above all others.

In terms of God, He operates at a level far above our own. He understands and sees things better than we ever could, and He is a better steward of our hopes and dreams. In Isaiah 55:9 God explains: "As the heavens are higher than the earth, so are My ways higher than your ways, and my thoughts than your thoughts." He knows that the greatest glory may not come by the route that we would expect.

In the 1924 Olympics, Harold Abrahams, a member of Great Britain's Olympic team, won the gold medal in the 100-meter race. Interestingly it is not Abrahams who is best remembered from this particular Olympics, or even in connection with this particular race. Rather it was one of his teammates, a Scotsman who was favored to win the race, who is remembered best. And this man did not even compete in the event. His name may not ring a bell, but if you were to sit down at a piano and plunk out C-F-G-A-G-E you may get an idea of his identity.

The movie *Chariots of Fire* chronicles the life of Scottish sprinter Eric Liddell. Liddell was the favorite to win the title of "fastest man on the planet" in the one hundred meter race in the 1924 Olympics. However, when he learned that the preliminaries were scheduled for a Sunday, he pulled out of the event, refusing to compete on the Lord's Day. In a biography of Liddell written by Eric Metaxas in the book *Seven Men*, the author comments on the amazing truth that "had Eric Liddell run that 100-meter race, as he was urged to do, he would be largely forgotten today outside of Scotland."[1] The only reason we even mention the gold medal winner Abrahams was because of his connection to Liddell.

The route to the greatest glory does not always come by the most obvious route. We remember Liddell because of the race he did not run and because of the potential gold medal which he passed up. We remember Hannah in the Bible because of the barrenness she struggled with prior to the birth of Samuel. The story of Joseph in the Bible is inspiring, not because of the heights to which he rose, but because of the depths from which he rose. The route to the greatest glory may not be as obvious as we expect.

Many refuse to entrust the stewardship of their lives into God's hands because they presume to know the best route to the greatest glory. This was not the case with the Apostle Paul. He declared, "I know whom I have believed and am persuaded that He is able to keep what I have committed to Him until that Day" (2

Timothy 1:12). At the heart of Paul's statement was the conviction that God would be a better steward than he himself. "I am persuaded that He is able," said the apostle.

Paul committed himself to the Lord without reservation because he was convinced that God had the ability and goodness to treat well what had been committed to His care. I believe that the goodness of God is the attribute that many of us struggle with most. We know that He has the ability to be a good steward, but does He have the goodness? Will He treat well what we have committed to Him? We will deal more with these questions later.

The Last Chapter

We noted a moment ago that we are inspired by the life of Joseph in the Bible because of the depths from which he rose. At the end of his life, as he looked back on the highly unpredictable route that had led to a high position in the Egyptian government, we find that Joseph had some very interesting perspective on what he had experienced. As his brothers stood before him, he said, "You meant evil against me; but God meant it for good, in order to bring it about as it is this day, to save many people alive" (Genesis 50:20).

After reviewing the entire book of his life, Joseph confessed that God had dealt well with him. This is the testimony of the righteous. With rare exceptions, those who remain unmoved despite the struggles of life confess at the end that God has been faithful.

But imagine with me if Joseph had responded differently to the pain and disappointment he experienced. What if he had succumbed to the struggle as a young man and turned away from the Lord? What if he had turned bitter against God after being wrongly imprisoned following the accusation by Potiphar's wife?

Would his testimony still have spoken of God's faithfulness? I think not. It would have certainly been one of God's failures and unfaithfulness.

The question to consider is this: Which Joseph would be able to more accurately speak to God's faithfulness, or lack thereof? Whose testimony would you believe: the Joseph who had remained faithful and seen the story through to the end, or the one who had walked away from the Lord mid-way through the book? Both would be equally convinced of their accuracy in judging God's activity in their lives.

David himself made an interesting comment that applies to this in Psalm 18:26. Referring to the Lord, he says: "With the pure You will show yourself pure; and with the devious You will show Yourself shrewd." David is explaining that our perception of God will be determined by our response to Him. Had Joseph walked away from the Lord in his seasons of trials, he would have perceived God as unfaithful.

In Psalm 139:16 we read, "In Your book they all were written, the days fashioned for me, when as yet there were none of them." Can you judge a book by its cover? Can you predict the end when you're only halfway through? And yet many judge God as unfaithful when only a handful of chapters have played out. In waiting until the book of his life had been fully read, Joseph had the perspective to accurately conclude that God had shown Himself faithful.

What about you? To this point, would you conclude that God has been faithful? Taking the principle we drew from Psalm 18:26, we could reword the passage to say: "With the unfaithful You will appear unfaithful; but with the faithful you will appear faithful." Your response to God has determined your perception of Him. He has promised that He will complete the good work the He began in you. Will you remain faithful to the process and allow the final chapters to be written?

In Acts 20:27, the Apostle Paul said to the elders of the church in Ephesus, "I have not shunned to declare to you the whole counsel of God." The whole counsel of God comes to us through two books. The first book is the Bible. In God's Word we find unfailing counsel regarding God's activity in our lives.

The second book takes far longer to read. It is the book of our lives. Noting the words of David once more, we read, "In Your book they all were written, the days fashioned for me."[2] To fully grasp what God is doing in your life, the entire book of your life must be allowed to unfold. You will not be able to write an accurate review of God's plan for you until the final chapter has played out.

I recall that following a particularly difficult season in the life of my family, a friend commented to me, "It must be difficult attempting to answer the question, 'Why?'" I responded that it is not hard to answer the question if you never ask it.

I believe that there are some questions that even God could not answer in two or three sentences. The reason being that for many questions, the answers are revealed over a lifetime. In such instances it may only be after the entire book of your life has unfolded that an answer can be discovered.

Solomon concludes the book of Ecclesiastes by urging his readers to "Hear the conclusion of the whole matter." You will not be able to understand the activity of God in your life until you have read the conclusion of the matter and allowed the course of your life to fully unfold.

I believe that the wind principle is one of the most exciting truths that could fill our hearts. "The wind blows where it wishes, and you hear the sound of it, but cannot tell where it comes from and where it goes. So is everyone who is born of the Spirit."

God wants to take you from an insignificant starting point along an unpredictable route to an unexpected, good destination. And the best part is that you do not have to provide the energy. The Spirit of God is the vehicle. You simply have to remain positioned to be moved. Let your heart expand today with the possibilities.

Lynchpin

GENERALLY you might expect to find the lynchpin of a concept toward the end of the process. In the case of the wind principle, we find it is at the outset. The wind principle rests on the last words of Jesus in John 3:8, "So it is with everyone who is born of the Spirit."

I recently noticed a Facebook post from a young lady who was upset by the trouble she was facing in life. She could not understand why after having been baptized as an infant and confirmed that she would continue to face so many set-backs and such opposition in life. She was hoping to experience a life that was moved along by God's Spirit to a good destination. Her experience was far different than what she had expected.

The problem was that the lynchpin was not in place in her life; she had no experience of having been born of the Spirit. The hinge on which the wind principle moves was not in place in her life, and she was not even aware of it. To that point her confidence was in religious ritual and tradition. We find in John 3 that Nicodemus was in a very similar place on the night he visited Jesus.

It seems likely that Nicodemus sought out Jesus, not as a representative of the Pharisees, but of his own accord. He was a sincere man who relied on religious ritual, ceremony and tradition for his confidence. Despite his credentials and knowledge, something moved him to seek out Jesus.

The Lord went right to the center of Nicodemus' need. In John 3:3 He says, "Most assuredly, I say to you, unless one is born again, he cannot see the kingdom of God."

This posed a couple immediate problems for Nicodemus. The first was that there were obvious physical limitations which prevented a strict literal application of what Jesus said. He responds to Christ, "How can a man be born when he is old? Can he enter a second time into his mother's womb and be born?" (John 3:4).

I believe that the more practical obstacle Nicodemus identified can be illustrated by an old *Far Side* cartoon by Gary Larson. The cartoon features a dog high in the air on a tight-rope riding a unicycle with a cat in his mouth while juggling four balls. He is half-way across the rope as the caption reads, "High above the hushed crowd Rex tried to remain focused. Still, he couldn't shake one nagging thought: He was an old dog and this was a new trick."

I believe that in his response Nicodemus is pointing toward the second and more practical problem that Jesus' command posed. He was an old dog. He had spent his life developing certain habits and attitudes that could not easily be changed. How was he to start over when he was old?

Jesus answers by expanding on His statement: "Unless one is born of water and the Spirit, he cannot enter the kingdom of God" (John 3:5). The type of rebirth that Jesus is speaking of is in no way natural, but spiritual. In fact He excludes any natural element when He says, "That which is born of the flesh is flesh, and that which is born of the Spirit is spirit."

Natural effort produces natural results. A child is born because a man and woman come together intimately. Flesh gives birth to flesh. Religion apart from the new birth provided by the Spirit is the same. It will always produce that which is natural.

Conversely, Jesus says that Spirit gives birth to spirit. Christ was not calling Nicodemus to try to start over or straighten up. Rather he was calling him to be born of the Spirit. No longer would Nicodemus' efforts produce fleshly results. Filled with the life given by God's Spirit, the produce of his life would now be spiritual in nature.

But someone may ask, "Why is it necessary that I be born again? Isn't it very narrow to suggest that entrance into God's kingdom would require new birth through Christ?" The answer is, "No." The need for new birth is not a matter of law but a matter of logistics.

In 1 Corinthians 15:50 Paul wrote, "Now this I say, brethren, that flesh and blood cannot inherit the kingdom of God." Our natural composition is flesh and blood. It is this natural composition that excludes us from a spiritual kingdom. We simply cannot inherit God's kingdom. To inherit God's kingdom our composition must be changed. Jesus was literally saying, "You *must* be born again." There is no other way to enter a spiritual kingdom.

The new birth also resolves the major issue that we all share in common with Nicodemus. How can we start over despite all of the behavior patterns and attitudes we have established over the course of our lives? In 2 Corinthians 5:17 we find the answer: "If anyone is in Christ, he is a new creation; old things have passed away; behold, all things have become new."

Once the lynchpin of the new birth is in place, the wind principle comes into play. Our lives will begin to be moved by God's Spirit from an unimpressive starting point along an unpredictable path toward an unexpected destination.

It is a path very similar to that which was taken by Jesus. His start was as insignificant as one could imagine. The path He took from His unimpressive beginning to His destination would never have been predicted. The Bible tells us that He took on the form of a servant. His destination, death on the cross, was certainly not expected by those who followed His life. Neither was His resurrection.

I have been unable to track down the source of this quote, but it is worth repeating:

> "Wherever Jesus appeared He impressed. The atmosphere was electric with all manner of possibilities. From a situation in which they found themselves He always emerged by a way which they would have never guessed."

If Christ lives in you, this is a commentary on your life. It is electric with all manner of possibilities. Irrespective of where you begin, you will later emerge at a place where neither you nor anyone else would have ever imagined.

Transforming Death

In Jerusalem, there are two locations which have been identified as possible locations of the crucifixion of Jesus. The traditional spot lies within the church of the Holy Sepulcher. An alternative location, known as "Gordon's Calvary", is named after the famed

British General Charles Gordon. Gordon was the most prominent early supporter of this being the place of Jesus' crucifixion. The site features a ridge which rises up from what is currently a bus station. The rocky features of the ridge give the appearance of the face of a skull.

In Jerusalem, a short walk from "Gordon's Calvary," there is an ancient tomb set in a garden. Many believe that this is the tomb where Jesus' body was temporarily housed. Regardless of the actual location of Jesus' burial, the reality is that this garden tomb, which was designed to be a place for the dead, has been transformed into a place of life and hope.

In Peter's sermon on the Day of Pentecost, he declared that God had raised up Jesus, "having loosed the pains of death, because it was not possible that He should be held by it" (Acts 2:24). The grave was undefeated and untied before Christ. David vs. Goliath analogies did not fit because the grave never lost. The effect of Christ's presence in the tomb was that life came to the place of death, but it was more than that. Peter says that it was not possible that there would be any other outcome.

Jesus has the effect of bringing life wherever He goes. The tomb was a place of death until Jesus entered. A funeral procession in the village of Nain was proceeding without incident until Christ happened to come along. Jesus has a way of rerouting hopeless situations from their expected outcome.

The effect of His presence upon your life will be that He will transform your places of death into places of life. Dead-end jobs, dead-end marriages, and dead-end dreams receive a new lease on life when Christ comes on the scene. How could it be any different? If Jesus lives in you, your life is electric with His life-giving potential.

Where He is present, it is impossible that death will retain its hold. This is the message of 1 Corinthians 15:54: "Death is swallowed up in victory."

One place that was not electric was Nazareth. In Mark 6:5 we read, "Now (Jesus) could do no mighty work there, except that He laid His hands on a few sick people and healed them."

Nazareth had the same Jesus, but not the same effect. The potential was there, but was not realized. In the next verse we find that the cause and culprit was unbelief. Rather than being a place electric with possibility, it was a place stagnant with skepticism.

No Dead Ends

As we read through the Gospels we frequently find Jesus' critics setting traps for Him. These frequently came in the form of a question with two possible answers, neither of which were good.

On one occasion He was asked, "Is it lawful to pay taxes to Caesar or not?"[1] Yes or no, those were the possible answers. To answer "yes" would turn the Jews against Him because it would suggest that the rule of the Romans was legitimate. To answer "no" would set Him against the Roman authorities, risking their condemnation. They gave Him two choices, neither of which was good.

On another occasion a woman was brought to Jesus who had been caught in the act of adultery.[2] They put the matter to His judgment: "The law says this woman should be stoned, what say you?" Two options: follow the law and have her stoned, or ignore the law and let her go.

On both occasions Jesus emerged in a way that was unexpected, leaving His opponents dumbfounded. Matthew 22:46 records that eventually, "no one dared question Jesus anymore" in such a way. They simply could not overcome or defeat His wisdom.

Satan will attempt to place us in a similar position. He will make it appear that a dead end is straight ahead, with only two bad options. When we come to a dead end, what are those options? We can stay where we are and make no more progress, or we can retrace our steps and lose valuable time. Satan will make you believe that those are the only possible choices, but the great news is that wherever Jesus is, there is always another way.

If He lives in you there are no dead ends. In 2 Samuel 22:20, David wrote, "He also brought me out into a broad place." Satan wants to constrain you. Jesus seeks to bring you out to a place where there is plenty of space to move and grow.

Where the lynchpin is in place the wind principle comes into effect. "So it is with everyone who is born of the Spirit." God's Spirit will move you from your insignificant starting points along an unpredictable path toward an unexpected destination.

Out of the Sheepfold

3

YOU may have lived in a community which has carried a less then flattering characterization. Jesus' hometown was that type of community. Skepticism was thick regarding anything which originated within the city limits of Nazareth. "Can anything good come out of Nazareth?"[1] were the first words out of Nathanael's mouth when he was told of Jesus' hometown.

The same thing would have been said about the origins of David. Can anything good come out of a sheepfold? Why even bother to present him to the prophet Samuel? Nothing great could come out of a place so insignificant.

In 2013 Wilfredo de Jesus, pastor of New Life Covenant Church in Chicago, was included in the Time 100 list of the most influential people in the world. The church he pastors is one of the largest Assemblies of God churches in the country and Pastor Choco, as he is better known, has become a national Hispanic leader.

In his book, *Amazing Faith*, he looked back at a pivotal moment early in his life when rioting and looting were taking place on the streets of Chicago. He writes of his response as a grocery store was being robbed: "I was caught up in the moment, but I could bring myself only to steal a bottle of soda pop from the refrigerator." Before walking off he stopped in his tracks and thought, "What in the world am I doing?" He concludes the story by commenting, "People who saw a confused kid take the bottle of soda pop back into the looted store during a riot would have likely asked, 'Can anything good come out of that boy's life?'"[2]

The effect of the wind principle is that God takes His choicest servants from the most unlikely places—like a sheepfold or a rioting city—and begins to move and direct their lives toward the destination which He has in mind. History has proven that He particularly enjoys choosing and using the most unlikely.

Rather than accepting the characterizations placed upon you because of your past, accept what the wind principle reveals. Your starting point has no bearing on God's selection process for great tasks. In fact, often the less qualified you appear, the more qualified you may well be, in God's estimation.

View from the Sheepfold

I wonder what David would have thought if he could have looked down from the shepherd fields outside of Bethlehem to watch his father proudly display his older brothers before the great prophet Samuel. Perhaps he would have thought about the simple beginnings of Joseph, the great-grandson of Abraham. He had been a cast-off among his brothers too, but at least Joseph had his father in his corner. In the case of David, it was his father Jesse who had chosen to leave him on the back forty when Samuel came to town.

As far as everyone was concerned, David was going nowhere. He was a good shepherd, and that was likely all he would ever be. Years later, when God was reviewing His activity in the life of Israel's second king, it seems that even He noted David's simple beginnings. He twice mentioned, *in the same sentence*, that when he had been chosen to be king, David had been out watching the sheep.[3]

The view from the sheepfold is not very impressive. From there we can often see those like David's brothers who tend to catch everyone's attention. Even Samuel, when he saw Eliab, the oldest of Jesse's sons, thought, "Surely the Lord's anointed is before Him!" (1 Samuel 16:6). There was certainly nothing wrong with having the personality or bearing that attracted attention, except that those were not the qualities God was seeking. In 1 Samuel 13:14, the prophet identifies the only must-have quality that God was looking for in a future king: "The Lord has sought for Himself a man after His own heart."

In the opening verses of Luke 3, we find a list of seven giants dotting the political landscape at the time of the ministry of John the Baptist. These seven men had spent their lives chasing after significance. They had schemed and maneuvered themselves for an opportunity to rise to the point where they held positions of power in the land. These men had the qualities that would attract attention. Yet it was not through these men that God would choose to speak. Luke writes, "The word of God came to John the son of Zacharias in the wilderness."[4] As author and speaker Ravi Zacharias once commented, "It was to a strange man, wearing strange clothes and eating strange food" that the word of the Lord came.

When it comes to the desire for significance, we can chase the wind or be moved by the Wind. Solomon wrote of chasing the wind in Ecclesiastes. He said, "I looked on all the works that my hands had done and on the labor in which I had toiled; and indeed all was vanity and grasping for the wind. There was no profit under the sun" (Ecclesiastes 2:11). Zacharias has pointed out that this phrase "under the sun" describes a life from which God has been shut out.

To shut God out and pursue significance is as futile as chasing after the wind. Frequently, those we notice from our view in the sheepfold will be those who are running in their own strength.

As the prophet looked Jesse's oldest son over, the Lord spoke to him saying, "Do not look at his appearance or at his physical stature, because I have refused him. For the Lord does not see as man sees, for man looks at the outward appearance, but the Lord looks at the heart" (1 Samuel 16:7). The finality of God's words to Samuel is striking: "I have refused him." He had no value for the task at hand. Why? The answer was: he did not have it where it counted. One can have everything the world values and yet lack the qualities sought by God.

This reality has a way of bringing perspective to our time in the sheepfold. Whose attention are you looking to attract? You may not have the charisma that will get the world to take notice of you, but you do have the opportunity to nurture the qualities that will cause God to take notice. While those around you chase the wind, determine to be that man or woman who God notices. Imagine how far you can go if you are being moved by the Wind rather than chasing the wind.

Self-Imposed Boundaries

I recall in high school experiencing a peculiar form of peer pressure. It was the pressure to remain in the middle of the pack. If you were too much different than the pack, either ahead or behind, you would feel the pressure. I was by no means a superior student, but I sensed the pressure to remain with the pack. David's courageous inquiries about Goliath set him outside the pack of scared Israelites soldiers. To get him back in their fold, they tried to tie him to his past.

In 1 Samuel 17, as David sought to rise out of the sheepfold, we find his oldest brother challenging him, saying, "With whom have you left those few sheep in the wilderness?" There are certainly more imposing fences which have been built than those constructed to pen in sheep, but there are few that are more difficult to escape.

As David sought to escape, those around him attempted to keep him tied to what he had always been. "You are a shepherd. You belong with the sheep."

I recently watched a television program which examined how the boundaries and shape of the states came to be. They told of an interesting situation on the border of Tennessee and Georgia which resulted in the current border being one mile further north than the U.S. Congress had originally designated. While the congressional designation was clear, the program stated that once a boundary is set on a map, it is very difficult to change.

Perhaps even more difficult to overcome than boundaries placed on us by others will be the boundaries we place upon ourselves. How far would David have gone if he would have accepted the contention that he would never be anything more than a simple shepherd? In Proverbs 23:7 we read, "As (a man) thinks in his heart, so is he." It is easy to restrict what God can do through us by the way we think of ourselves.

The prophet Jeremiah struggled with self-imposed boundaries. Early in the first chapter of his book we read of the prophetic call he received: "Then the word of the Lord came to me, saying, 'Before I formed you in the womb I knew you; before you were born I sanctified you; I ordained you a prophet to the nations'" (Jeremiah 1:4-5).

Jeremiah's immediate reaction to God's call was to construct self-imposed boundaries based on the way he perceived his own abilities. When called he responded to God, "Ah, Lord God! Behold, I cannot speak, for I am a youth."[5] Jeremiah saw his age as a boundary to the calling. In the case of Moses, as he interacted with God at the burning bush, it was his oratory skills, or lack thereof, that Moses saw as a boundary to the calling. To step into the call of God, both of these men would need to move beyond self-imposed boundaries.

What does it mean to escape these boundaries? Would it mean that David should have begun to see himself as having king-potential? In Romans 12:3, the Apostle Paul answers such questions, explaining that we should not view ourselves more highly than we ought. Overcoming self-imposed boundaries means that we accept that God can overcome any deficiency in our own ability. It means that we unhinge ourselves from our perceived limitations on the merit of God's abilities.

To overcome such boundaries we will need a heart that is enlarged to embrace God possibilities. In 1 Kings 4:29 we read that along with wisdom and understanding, God gave Solomon "largeness of heart like the sand on the seashore." What is possible for your life if the destination depends, not on you, but on God?

What we find at the heart of the wind principle is that it does not depend upon us. It is the Spirit who does the moving.

As we embrace the truths within the wind principle, our hearts will be enlarged to embrace what is possible through God. It does not matter where you have come from or where you are currently. The wind will blow, and it will not be restrained. If our heart is in a place where it can be moved, then God's Spirit will take us to the unexpected destination.

In Luke 1:37 we pick up this simple statement: "With God nothing will be impossible." The context of this passage is the angel Gabriel's visit to Mary bringing the news of two coming miraculous births. Mary's relative Elizabeth would bear a son in her old age, and Mary herself, a virgin, would give birth to God's Son. The angel told Mary of the special plans God had for His Son, explaining, "He will be great."

Mary responded to the announcement in a very logical way: "How can this be, since I do not know a man?" Mary knew that because she had never been in an intimate relationship with a man, she lacked what was needed to bear a child. The seed was not in her. The angel replied, "The Holy Spirit will come upon you, and the power of the Highest will overshadow you" (Luke 1:35). The birth of God's Son would come about through the power of the Holy Spirit.

The design that God has for your life is great, as it was for His Son. He intends to move you by His Spirit toward a destination that is in line with His nature. His plan for you is good. Like Mary you may consider such a possibility and question, "How can such a thing be? I do not have within me what is needed to bring about such an outcome." You may feel that you lack the charisma or discipline that is essential. The answer of the angel to Mary is the answer of God to you. It will be by the Spirit that you will reach the place of God's call.

The angel told Mary, "With God nothing will be impossible." When you believe God, it will become *impossible* for Him to do *nothing*. He's going to do something that no one would have expected.

No one would have guessed that anything good could come out of Nazareth. No one would have predicted that the second king of Israel would come out of a sheepfold. No one can predict the ways in which God will move in your life. What is He going to do? Who knows? But if you will believe God, nothing will become impossible.

Purpose in Obscurity

In ancient Israel there was possibly no more common profession than that of a shepherd. By its nature it would have felt like the most insignificant place in the world, especially when the country was at war.

During my first four years in pastoral ministry, I spent far more time at a local grocery store than I did in the church. I started out as a part-time student minister for the church, working about thirty hours a week outside the church. I remember the futility I felt at times while stocking shelves and carrying out groceries. It was a sheepfold time for me.

While the sheepfold seems insignificant, it is in reality a time of great opportunity. Those four years provided me with the opportunity to ease into ministry expectations. There were also many occasions when the soup aisle or coffee section provided some great ministry opportunities. I remember one particular occasion praying with one of the store managers about a back injury he was battling. When I said, "Amen" his eyes lit up as he exclaimed, "My back just popped!"

God does not waste any experience. The time you spend in the places that seem the most insignificant will be some of the most critical parts in the process of His development within your life.

The qualities that positioned David to be moved by the Spirit were first developed in the sheepfold while no one else was around. On the practical side of things, it was his ability with the harp and the sling that made him useful to Saul's kingdom. What was he doing those many hours while the sheep grazed? It was certainly a time when he progressed as a musician and songwriter. He also would have spent many hours picking off targets with the sling and the stone. He could not have seen the encounter with the giant in his future, but he knew there would be predators that would go after his sheep.

It is important to note that in the sheepfold, David's dependence on God grew in proportion to the growth of his ability. This is a critical point in our own development. The tendency is that as our skill increases, our dependence upon God decreases. This was the pattern in Saul's life. He began with the feeling that he was wholly inadequate for the calling. Within two years of taking the throne of Israel, Saul's relationship with God was little more than a tool to retain the favor of the people.

In the case of David, by the time he faced Goliath he was a crack-shot with the sling. In terms of skill, he probably possessed all he needed to kill the giant. But when the time came to face the giant, rather than leaning on his own ability, he said, "The battle is the Lord's, and He will give you into our hands."[6] He may have possessed the ability to defeat the giant, but he determined that any victory he accomplished would come through dependence on the Lord.

In John 15:5, Jesus says something critical, explaining, "Without Me you can do nothing." Several verses later He speaks of producing "fruit that lasts." This goes back to what Jesus told Nicodemus as He drew a contrast between what is produced by the flesh and what is produced by the Spirit of God.

A move away from dependence on God will invariably lead you away from what can be accomplished through God. When I lean on my abilities, I limit myself to the potential within myself. Why? The answer goes back to what we noted previously—fleshly efforts will never produce anything more than fleshly results. For this reason it is critical that our dependence upon God increases in proportion to an increase in our abilities and opportunities.

In the sheepfold David grew in courage. The victories against the bear and lion, which may have seemed insignificant at the time, added courage and confidence to the arsenal he would later need. Without those experiences to draw on, he would never have been able to step up to the challenge of facing the giant.

In the sheepfold David also grew in the area of worship. His practice of drawing near to God in worship would be indispensable later in life when he was being threatened by Saul, Absalom and the Philistines.

Without question, a number of the Psalms he wrote found their origin back in those early days. Imagine all the Psalms that may never have been written, had David had not spent those years in obscurity.

In 1 Peter 1:18-19 we read that we have been redeemed out of "aimless conduct" by the "precious blood of Christ." Meaningless experiences came to an end when you were born again. You have been redeemed out of that way of life. If you are currently in the sheepfold, you are there for a purpose. There are things that God intends to develop in you, to prepare you for life beyond the place of perceived insignificance.

When Jesse first sent David out to watch the sheep, he did so with a couple simple commands. David was to feed and protect the flock. The expectations were pretty basic. David would have had some extra time on his hands. Imagine the trouble David would have been in when he stepped out against Goliath if he had spent all that free time complaining about his situation, rather than sharpening his skill with the sling.

In Ecclesiastes 10:10 we read, "If the ax is dull, and one does not sharpen the edge, then he must use more strength; but wisdom brings success." How would you assess your abilities in the areas to which God has called you? If the ax is dull you are going to have to work twice as hard to get the job done. Take advantage of the lighter expectations within the sheepfold to sharpen your abilities in the areas of your calling.

Do not sit at home waiting for the exit door of the sheepfold to open for you. If you will take the time to sharpen your ax now when the expectations are low, you will be prepared when opportunities beyond the sheepfold arise.

The Right Track

While I was a student at Trinity Bible College in Ellendale, N.D., Rev. Charles Crabtree visited the campus. He was at that time the Assistant General Superintendent of the Assemblies of God and he spoke of discerning the will of God. He stated, "God generally does not rub the cat in the wrong direction." He was explaining that in dealing with us, God's will is generally in the direction of our abilities and desires. What does this mean for us?

When God found David, he was taking care of sheep for his father Jesse. Through His operation in David's life, God would raise the keeper of sheep to the throne of Israel where he would serve as a shepherd over the nation. David was always a shepherd. What changed was that God brought far greater purpose and nobility to the task of shepherding.

In Luke 5 we read of the miraculous catch of fish on the Sea of Galilee. Peter, James and John had fished all night and caught nothing. At Jesus' simple instruction, they obeyed and cast their net on the opposite side of the boat. The result was an incredible catch of fish.

Amazed at what had happened, Peter fell on his knees in front of Jesus, saying, "Depart from me, for I am a sinful man, O Lord!" Jesus responded, "Do not be afraid. From now on you will catch men." Peter would always be a fisherman, though now with far greater purpose. His redefined purpose would bring eternal significance to his life.

Where will God's Spirit take you as you experience the effect of the wind principle? The route will be unpredictable and the destination unexpected, but it will not necessarily be to a place entirely foreign to what you currently know. David was always a shepherd, but rather than shepherding sheep, he became a shepherd of people. Peter would always be a fisherman, but rather than catching fish, he began catching people. God will take what you currently possess and move you to a place where your skills and abilities are used for a more significant purpose.

Think for a moment about the fruit of Peter's worldly profession as a fisherman. He would catch fish and sell them at market. The money he received in return would allow him to purchase things important to his life and business. At the same time, these purchases would ultimately perish over time and with use. In bringing a higher calling to Peter's profession as a fisherman, God would enable him to bear fruit that would last into eternity.

The Lord desires to do the same for you. In John 15:16 Jesus said that we have been chosen and appointed to bear fruit that will remain. You can spend your life working for things that will perish with use, or you can accept God's call to a higher purpose.

The Secret Place

* 4 *

MORE is accomplished in the place of obscurity than we can imagine. We already noted that in the case of David, it was in the sheepfold where he honed his skills with the harp and the sling. Out of the public eye his spiritual life developed as he grew in worship and in faith. God's greatest work in David's life was completed outside of the public eye.

Another work accomplished in secret is the development of an unborn child. Nine months prior to birth, at the moment of conception, the genetic make-up of the baby is complete. Apart from cases of identical twins, an entirely unique human being has been created at that moment. Over the process of the following thirty-eight weeks, that original, unique cell will divide countless times to the point that a fully-developed baby will possess an estimated 3 to 4 trillion cells.

The entire process, from conception to the moment prior to birth, takes place in private, out of the public eye. David commented on the process in the 139th Psalm:

"You formed my inward parts; You covered me in my mother's womb. I will praise You, for I am fearfully and wonderfully made; marvelous are Your works, and that my soul knows very well. My frame was not hidden from You, when I was made in secret, and skillfully wrought in the lowest parts of the earth. Your eyes saw my substance, being yet unformed. And in Your book they all were written, the days fashioned for me, when as yet there were none of them" (Psalm 139:13-16).

Despite the incredible advance of science, many elements of the process of a baby's development remain a mystery. One such mystery is the function of embryonic stem cells. These particular cells appear within the first week following conception and possess the ability to form any tissue within the body. It is said that these cells "know" what to become. But how do they know? This is one of the mysteries surrounding the development of a child within the womb.

Similarly, the way that God will move in your life by the wind of His Spirit is mysterious. Solomon connects these two mysteries in Ecclesiastes 11:5, as he says, "As you do not know what is the way of the wind, or how the bones grow in the womb of her who is with child, so you do not know the works of God who makes everything."

Occasionally a child is born prematurely. When this is the case, special care must be taken because each step of prenatal development was to have been completed within the secret place of the womb. In your spiritual development, the most critical elements must also be completed within the secret place.

David said, "My frame was not hidden from You, when I was made in secret, and skillfully wrought in the lowest places of the earth. Your eyes saw my substance, being yet unformed." We generally apply this passage only to the development of a child, but I believe there is also an application here to spiritual development.

In Matthew 6:6, Jesus said, "When you pray, go into your room, and when you have shut your door, pray to your Father who is in the secret place; and your Father who sees in secret will reward you openly." It is only within the secret place of prayer that critical spiritual formation will take place. Without this time of formation we may emerge from the sheepfold immature and unprepared to complete what God has planned.

David said that his development within the secret place began when he was "yet unformed." This is how we began spiritually. We do not have a wealth of experience to draw upon. We may have not yet learned how to grasp spiritual concepts, nor do we yet know how to fully apply spiritual truths to our daily experiences. We are unformed. Does God despise our condition? No more than He does an unformed child.

The Psalmist noted that he was "skillfully wrought." In the secret place of the mother's womb a child is put together with great skill by the processes built in and overseen by God. It will be in the secret place of prayer that God's skill and care will be at work in your spiritual development.

Science has inserted itself into just about every aspect of human reproduction. Even then, there are aspects of the process which cannot be altered. One such aspect is the reality that the secret place of a mother's womb remains the only place where the pre-natal stages of human development can take place. Similarly, the secret place of prayer remains the only place where essential spiritual formation can take place.

No Shortcuts

Another aspect of reproduction that has remained unaltered by science is the length of gestation. It is still thirty-eight weeks from conception to the birth of a fully developed baby. Again, there are no shortcuts to the spiritual formation that God has planned for your life. Such progress can only occur within the place of prayer. There is no app that will provide you with a quicker route to spiritual maturity. It comes through time spent in prayer.

Though there are no shortcuts to what is accomplished in the secret place, Satan will still suggest that they exist. He is always suggesting shortcuts to the promise. In Genesis 12:1-3, God promised Abraham that he would be the father of a great people. Ten years later, and barren as ever, Sarah suggested to Abraham a shortcut to the promise. She told him, "See now, the Lord has restrained me from bearing children. Please, go in to my maid (Hagar); perhaps I shall obtain children by her" (Genesis 16:2). Abraham took the shortcut and within a year little Ishmael was born. This shortcut caused great problem within Abraham's house.

We find another shortcut offered, though rejected, in the temptation of Jesus. In Luke 4:5-7 we read, "Then the devil, taking Him up on a high mountain, showed Him all the kingdoms of the world in a moment of time. And the devil said to Him, 'All this authority I will give You, and their glory…if You will worship before me."

Would Satan have delivered? We can be certain that he would not have delivered. His shortcuts are never as advertised. But more significantly, the Father had already promised Jesus everything that Satan now offered in this temptation. In Psalm 2:7-8 we read, "The Lord has said to me, 'You are My Son, today I have begotten You. Ask of Me, and I will give You the nations for Your inheritance, and the ends of the earth for your possession."

Satan offered Jesus a route to the promise that avoided the cross. He does the same with us. He offers a path that requires no self-control, no self-denial, and no investment in prayer. But as with all of his paths, they never lead where promised. There is no substitute or shortcut to what is accomplished in the secret place of prayer.

Value in Obscurity

The time spent in places that may seem insignificant are significant because it provides the opportunity for genuine formation. When Jesus spoke of the importance of finding a secret place of prayer, He did so after noting the tendency of certain religious people to make a show of their prayer life. He explained:

> "When you pray, you shall not be like the hypocrites. For they love to pray standing in the synagogues and on the corners of the streets, that they may be seen by men. Assuredly, I say to you, they have their reward" (Matthew 6:5).

Jesus was pointing out that it is difficult for anything genuine to be accomplished in the spotlight. This is what makes the places of insignificance so significant. When you are seen by no one but God, everything that takes place is real. In Hebrews 4:13 we read, "All things are naked and open to the eyes of Him to whom we must give account." In the secret place there is no point pretending because God sees everything anyway.

It has been rightly said that it does not matter what is seen in public, the real you is the one in private. This is true in both the negative and positive sense. One can look good in public but be full of filth in the inner room of the heart. Or one can appear small and insignificant in the public eye but have a thriving inner room of prayer.

While David was in obscurity developing a heart after God, his more impressive brothers were being paraded before the prophet Samuel. In 2 Chronicles 16:9 we read, "The eyes of the Lord run to and fro throughout the whole earth, to show Himself strong on behalf of those whose heart is loyal to Him."

As the eyes of the Lord ran to and fro over these two scenes, He took notice of the obscure shepherd with a heart after God. Be encouraged to take a lesson from this, and commit yourself to developing the inner self in the secret place of prayer.

The Reward of the Secret Place

What is the reward of time spent in prayer? Today's teachers suggest that the purpose of prayer is not to receive from God or see things change, but rather to bring our hearts in line with the will of God. I believe this teaching misleads us as to the true purpose of prayer on several levels.

First, it is certainly important that our heart come into line with the will of God. However this is not the purpose of prayer. Rather it is the by-product of prayer. In Psalm 37:4 we read, "Delight yourself also in the Lord, and He shall give you the desires of your heart." The effect of prayer and communion with God is that He places His desires within our heart. As we pray our heart realigns itself with God's heart.

Additionally, it is certain that if we pray with no expectation, we will receive nothing from God. James says as much when he states that the man who expects to receive nothing from God should not suppose that he will receive anything.[1]

In Hebrews 11:6 we read, "Without faith it is impossible to please Him, for he who comes to God must believe that He is, and that He is a rewarder of those who diligently seek Him." Notice here that an essential element of faith is the belief that God answers prayer. When we no longer expect God to respond to prayer, we have lost that which is at the very heart of faith. It could be said that if we do not expect to receive from God, our faith is incomplete.

Finally, we find throughout Scripture that God responds to prayer. Jesus said, "Ask, and it will be given to you; seek and you will find; knock, and it will be opened to you" (Matthew 7:7). The implication of this verse is that the door will remain closed unless one knocks.

I believe that the questionable teaching surrounding prayer comes from the disappointment that arises when prayers seem to go unanswered. Because we struggle to find an answer, we conclude that our theology must be wrong. We then begin to look for an explanation that fits our experience.

Much of the struggle could be avoided if we would intentionally submit our requests to the will of God, rather than attempting to mold our beliefs so that they fit our experience. In 1 John 5:14 we read, "This is the confidence that we have in Him, that if we ask anything according to His will, He hears us." The implication is that if our requests are outside His will, we will not receive what we have sought.

In December of 2010, my wife and I welcomed our daughter Malley Jo into our family. At her two week check-up the doctor commented that her skin appeared to be jaundiced. Four weeks later my wife took her in again because the discoloration remained. Blood tests ran at that appointment suggested the possibility of a serious liver condition.

Over the next several days doctors determined that she had been born with a condition that resulted in liver disease. Eight months later Malley was listed on the organ donor recipient list to receive a liver transplant.

I recall one evening calling out to God in prayer for her healing. I expressed to God that my request was not that she be made well by a transplant, but that it would be by His healing hand. In fact, I explained to God, I had no interest in having her receive a transplant.

A short time later I came upon Psalm 68:20 which reads: "Our God is the God of salvation; and to God the Lord belong escapes from death." This passage spoke to my heart in two ways. First it expressed to me that the method of my daughter's escape from death, be that by a miracle or a transplant, was God's to choose. Second, it revealed to me that regardless of the method chosen, the escape was something that would come from God. The Lord was calling me to submit my request to His method.

We find a model of this in the story of Shadrach, Meshach and Abednego in the Old Testament book of Daniel. In their expression of faith as they stood up to King Nebuchadnezzar, I see as complete a model of prayer and faith as is found anywhere in the Bible.

These three, along with Daniel, were among those taken captive from Jerusalem to Babylon when the Jewish capital was invaded by the Babylonians in 605 B.C. Sometime after the captives settled into life in Babylon, King Nebuchadnezzar erected an image in his own honor in the city.

Calling his officials together, the king commanded that all bow before the image at the sound of the music. These three men defied the command of the king, refusing to bow to the image. Responding to Nebuchadnezzar's reaction of outrage and rights over their defiant stance, they said:

> "Our God whom we serve is able to deliver us from the burning fiery furnace, and He will deliver us from your hand, O king. But if not, let it be known to you, O king, that we do not serve your gods, nor will we worship the gold image which you have set up" (Daniel 3:17-18).

Their bold statement hit the mark when it comes to authentic faith. They knew that God was able to deliver them, and they fully expected that He would. We can all have that level of faith; believing that God is able and expecting that He will.

But these men did not stop there. In their final words to the king before being cast into the fire, they made it clear that their prayer was submitted to the will of God. "But if not..." they added.

I believe that God would have us take the approach of Shadrach, Meshach, and Abednego every time we pray. We believe God is able and that He will! But I also believe that God desires we leave room for, "But if not." A biblical theology of prayer will include the confident belief that God is able and that He is a rewarder of those who seek Him. It will also include room for God to work in an unexpected manner.

Travel ahead with me now in the narrative of Scripture several hundred years to the time of the Early Church. The fledgling church was reeling in the wake of the merciless outbreak of persecution, unleashed after the martyrdom of Stephen. In Acts 8:1 we catch up with church historian Luke as he writes, "At that time a great persecution arose against the church which was at Jerusalem."

If we could go back to Jerusalem during this period of persecution, we would doubtless find groups of believers praying that God would bring an end to the attacks facing the church. They would plead with God for mercy. They would remind God of the great opportunities before them, and the way that persecution would threaten what was being accomplished. Yet, in spite of their prayers, we learn that the intense opposition continued. The book of Acts tells us that the result was: "they were all scattered throughout the regions of Judea and Samaria."

During that season the church must have struggled to see God's purpose in allowing the persecution to continue. They may have reasoned within themselves, "What a great testimony of God's power it would have been had God brought this to an end."

But years later when Luke documented the effect of the persecution, he noted: "Therefore those who were scattered (by persecution) went everywhere preaching the word."[2] The effect of the persecution was to get the church back on task. They had been called to be witnesses in "Judea and Samaria and to the ends of the earth." Instead, they had remained in Jerusalem, formed a tightly knit community of faith, all the while neglecting the command to extend their reach.

What would have been to that group of believers a difficult to understand unanswered prayer, we clearly see now as a part of God's plan to spread the Gospel beyond Jerusalem.

If we were to fast-forward in time a few more decades, I suspect we would come upon another prayer meeting. The focus of this particular gathering would have been upon the situation facing the Apostle Peter. Church history tells us that in the middle of the seventh decade after the birth of Christ, Peter was imprisoned by the Roman Emperor Nero, who had every intention of executing the apostle.

As the church prayed, they certainly would have had every expectation that God would answer. After all, He had done so before on behalf of Peter. In the twelfth chapter of Acts we find him imprisoned and the church gathered to offer "constant prayer...to God for him."[3] By the end of that chapter, Peter is free and the church is rejoicing at the miraculous deliverance.

I can imagine the way some of those prayers during this latest imprisonment may have been framed: "Lord, the church needs Peter's continued leadership." "God, deliver Peter for the sake of your glory and as a testimony of your power." After all, they may have reasoned, it certainly would not be God's will that Peter die.

As daylight came on the day of the scheduled execution, word came that Nero's plan had indeed been carried out and that their beloved Peter was now dead. This unanswered prayer would not have made any sense at the time. But to this day we look at the willingness of the apostles to die for their faith as the strongest evidence for the resurrection of Jesus. This unanswered prayer serves as one of the foundational arguments for our Christian faith.

Here are two instances when there was incredible purpose behind unanswered prayers. And yet that purpose would have been hidden from those within the church at that time. The point is, there is much we do not see or understand.

When we allow unanswered prayers to greatly trouble our faith, it suggests that we believe we can judge in the present what often can only be seen clearly from a distance. Remember, the wind principle teaches we cannot predict the destination based on our current position.

I cannot tell you what God is up to in the midst of unanswered prayers, but I can tell you that whatever it is, it will be good. So keep trusting and keep praying, and watch God develop in you the qualities essential to your destination.

The Fuel

5

THERE has likely not been a more unimpressive beginning than that found in the opening verses of the Bible. In Genesis 1:1-2 we read, "In the beginning God created the heavens and the earth. The earth was without form, and void; and darkness was on the face of the deep. And the Spirit of God was hovering over the face of the waters." This was certainly not the way the earth was created to exist. In Isaiah 45:18 we read that God did not create it to be empty, but rather, to be inhabited. Yet here it was lacking definition and resources.

Over this situation hovered the Spirit of God. The agent of God's action was on the scene, and yet the earth remained a place of formless emptiness. In Genesis 1:3 things get moving as God says, "Let there be light." Suddenly the darkness that had engulfed the surface of the deep dissolved as light burst onto the scene. Over the following verses the world and universe as we know it took shape as the Father spoke the Word into an atmosphere in which the Spirit of God was present.

With every creative act we read, "And God said." In every instance the creative energy required to move the earth from the unimpressive emptiness of its beginnings to its intended purpose as a place which could be inhabited hinged on the Word of God. What would have happened had God never spoken? What if He had never said, "Let there be light"?

Despite the creative power and energy of the Holy Spirit, creation would not have happened without the Word of God, which John the Apostle identifies as none other than Jesus Himself. In the opening verses of his Gospel, we read, "In the beginning was the Word, and the Word was with God, and the Word was God...And the Word became flesh and dwelt among us" (John 1:1, 14).

The Spirit of God did not work independent of the Word of God. I believe that it is reasonable to assume that if the Word had not been spoken, the earth would have remained formless and void. It was the addition of the Word of God into an atmosphere rich with the Spirit of God that unleashed creative power.

In John 16:5-15 Jesus provides us with critical information about the operation of God's Spirit. He explains that the Spirit will not "speak on His own authority."[1] Rather He will communicate only what He receives from the Father or from the Son. The reason for the deferential nature of God's Spirit is expressed in the next verse where Jesus says, "He will glorify Me."

Creation awaited the addition of the Word of God because the Spirit desired to bring glory to the Son. Because the creative activity of the Spirit waited on the addition of the Word, we now read in John 1:3, "All things were made through (the Word), and without Him nothing was made that was made." The Son received the glory for Creation.

So we have the unimpressive earth, formless and void, taking shape and becoming what it was designed to be, a place to be inhabited. All this took place when the Word of God was added to an atmosphere in which the Spirit of God was present.

If we could have viewed the earth in Genesis 1:2 in its uninhabitable state, we would have never been able to determine its purpose. We would never have guessed that it had been made to be inhabited. Neither would we have been able to identify any hope for anything different, because it lacked any resources with which purpose could take shape. If the Word of God had never been spoken over the formless expanse of earth, nothing would have changed.

I'd like to draw some comparisons between a person, newly born of the Spirit, and the state in which we find the earth in Genesis 1:2. As was true of the earth at this particular stage, so it is true of an individual who has just been born again. There may be little to hint at or suggest what God's ultimate purpose may be for this "new creation." Others may look at this person and see no obvious natural resources with which a divine purpose could take shape. What that individual does possess is the Holy Spirit, waiting to take that one from his or her unimpressive beginning to an unexpected destination.

In Genesis 1:3 it was the introduction of God's Word into the atmosphere rich with God's Spirit which released creative power. It is the same in terms of the Spirit's activity in your life. He awaits the addition of God's Word.

If you want to see the Holy Spirit do something exciting in your life, you must fill yourself with the Word, by reading the Bible. When God's Word is added to the atmosphere of your life, creative power is unleashed. The Spirit is the vehicle of the wind principle, but the Word of God is the fuel.

John explains, as we previously noted, that apart from the Word, "nothing was made that was made." It was the Word that brought light to the darkness. It was the Word that caused dry ground to appear, providing a foundation for the rest of Creation. Similarly, it is the Word that will bring form and purpose to your life.

The Spirit will only work in concert with the Word. Without its addition into your life, nothing will be made that could be made. The effect of the wind principle will not be experienced apart from God's Word.

And There Was Light

When I was in high school my history teacher assigned each student an oral report on a historical figure. I was assigned the 19th-century German philosopher, Friedrich Nietzsche. The teacher knew that I was the son of a pastor and a believer in Christ. I suspect that he was interested to hear my perspective on this antagonist of religious faith.

Apparently Nietzsche's philosophy was beyond me at that time. I do not recall anything noteworthy from the report I gave. Although I missed the significance of his life, Nietzsche continues to have a profound influence on modern thought.

The movie *God's Not Dead*, released in 2014, was a response to the notion that God *is* dead, which was first popularized by Nietzsche in the 19th century. He believed that God had become philosophically irrelevant, and was by all accounts dead. He maintained that rationalism and science had shut God out of the picture.

It is interesting to note that the rationalism of the 1800's has now been displaced by the irrationalism of post-modern thought. In addition, the advances of science now point toward the need of explanations which only God can provide. One author has written: "The whole field of origin of life studies is in a quandary. All the old theories have broken down; no acceptable new theory is on the horizon. The origin of life seems inexplicable."[2] Facing the evidence suggesting that God alone can explain the existence of the universe and life, naturalistic scientists are forced to constantly remind themselves that what they see is not the result of design.[3]

Nietzsche may not have spoken with such confidence about the supposed death of God had he possessed the knowledge provided by modern science. What he did possess was an understanding of what man would face following the eviction of God from his consciousness. In his allegorical *Parable of the Madman* he suggested that as a result of "the death of God", man would now need to light lanterns in the morning.[4]

When we open the Bible, the first words spoken by God were, "Let there be light." The effect of God's Word was to bring light. I think it is interesting to note that the first effect Nietzsche identified following the philosophical "death of God" was the lack of light. He was aware that natural light alone was insufficient for man.

In Psalm 119:105 we read, "Your word is a lamp to my feet and a light to my path." The addition of God's Word to your life provides the light you need as a guide for your steps. It will show you where to step when your feelings threaten to mislead you. If the Word is absent, darkness will dominate.

When God's Word was spoken over creation, it responded. How amazing then to consider that man can set his will against the Word of God, refusing to respond. If the Word is to fuel the wind principle, there must be a submission on our part to its authority. We must trust it more than we trust ourselves.

Paul explained this to his young protégé Timothy when he wrote, "You must continue in the things which you have learned and been assured of, knowing from whom you have learned them, and that from childhood you have known the Holy Scriptures, which are able to make you wise for salvation through faith which is in Christ Jesus" (2 Timothy 3:14-15). What do you do when you don't know which direction to turn? Stick with what you have known. Lean on those whose example you trust. Go to the well from which your spiritual fathers drew.

The wind principle is on track in my life today because many years ago I submitted to the instruction of this passage. A series of experiences had left me confused and troubled. I felt like I was being pulled in two totally different directions, and I had no idea to which direction I should release control. I felt totally lost as I sat in my cabin at Bible camp one summer when God's Word lit the path ahead: "Continue in the things which you have learned…knowing from whom you have learned them." I couldn't trust my feelings, but I felt I could trust those who had taught me about Christ, so I continued in what I had learned. It was a giant moment in my life.

In such moments, we need something we can draw on. In Psalm 119:11, we read, "Your Word I have hidden in my heart, that I might not sin against You." God's Word provides us with the reserves we will need when those moments come.

A Good Foundation

On the third creation day[5] we find that God spoke and dry land appeared. This provided the foundation for the rest of his creative works. Without the Word there would have been nothing on which life could have been supported.

A good foundation is extremely important. An athlete needs the foundation provided by strong, healthy legs to compete. A building needs a solid foundation to remain structurally sound. In life, the need of a solid foundation is equally important.

In Psalm 119:130, we read, "The entrance of Your words gives light; it gives understanding to the simple." The Word gives understanding where it was lacking. It places something *under* us on which we can *stand*. It gives us a foundation on which our lives can be built. Without the Word, there will be nothing to support life.

Just as the addition of the Word in Genesis 1:9 caused dry land to appear which would support plant and animal life, and ultimately human life, so the addition of the Word to your life provides a foundation to support God's creative activity in you.

Pray Before You Read

In Luke 11:1, Jesus' disciples come to him with a request: "Lord, teach us to pray." They were essentially praying that Jesus would teach them to pray.

Going to the longest chapter in the Bible, we find a similar request: "Open my eyes, that I may see wondrous things from Your law" (Psalm 119:18). The author knew that wonderful things could be found in God's Word. Perhaps this knowledge came by personal experience or by the testimony of others; regardless he started out by praying for eyes to see what was within God's Word.

Notice that the author did not complain that the "wondrous things" were too hard to find. The problem was not in the revelation but in his ability to see. If a blind man is unable to see the sun, he does not complain about the sun but attempts to address the issue of his vision.

I am always saddened when people complain that they receive nothing from God's Word. When that is the case, it is not that the revelation is too complex, but that our own vision is too poor. We need to pray for spiritual vision which will allow us to comprehend what is found in God's Word.

When it comes to the Word of God, something extremely valuable has been discovered. If we receive nothing from it, the issue is not the difficulty of the revelation but our lack of diligence in searching it out. To find what is present we should follow the example of the Psalmist, and pray, "Open my eyes, that I may see wondrous things in Your Word."

In the Old Testament book of 2nd Kings, the servant of the prophet Elisha awakens one morning to find that he and the prophet are surrounded by the Syrian army.[6] Fearing for his life the servant asks Elisha, "What shall we do?" Elisha calmly responds, "Do not fear, for those who are with us are more than those who are with them."

Based only on what the servant was seeing, Elisha's comment made no sense. That is, until the prophet prays, "Lord...open his eyes that he may see." When his eyes were opened, the Bible says, "He saw. And behold, the mountain was full of horses and chariots of fire all around Elisha." The horses and chariots of fire were there all along, but they were only seen when spiritual vision was given. What the servant then saw made all the difference.

God's Word is full of wondrous things that will make all the difference in your life. If you are not finding those things, the issue is that vision is lacking. Before you read, ask God to open your eyes to see wondrous things that you would otherwise miss.

Across from our home there is a park with a newly laid quarter-mile walking path. This past fall I was walking this path on a cool October morning. As I returned home I caught sight of the morning sunlight shining through the fall colored trees. In the foreground were dozens of pumpkins that our neighbor had set out to sell. My first thought was that it was the type of scene that a good photographer would have liked to have captured.

Yet even the best photographer could not have done the scene justice. The photograph would have missed the brilliance of the sun through the trees and the scene behind me as the sun rose on the hills rising up from the valley. It would have also missed the feeling of the cool fall air and the smell of the falling cottonwood leaves. In short the image captured by the best photographer would have been very limited in comparison to that which I gained by firsthand experience.

I have come across many who tell me that they seldom read the Bible for themselves. They explain that their source for devotional reading is limited to what others have written. They will read a short devotional consisting of a few verses of Scripture and an author's thoughts, and call that good.

Devotional readings can be great tools that can add to our experience, but if this is the extent of our exposure to God's Word, we limit our vision to what God has given to someone else. Just as a photo cannot provide the full scope of what a scene reveals, you will never receive the full scope of what God hopes to communicate to you by reading only what others have written. The Word is complemented by what others write, but it cannot be replaced by what they write, no matter how skilled they may be.

God has something He wants to reveal to you in His Word. I encourage you to prayerfully begin reading God's Word for yourself today. He has something He wants to say to you!

Section 2: An Unpredictable Route

The Stronghold of En Gedi, circa 1036 B.C.

"Tell the men to prepare to push forward. We will focus our energy at the center of the enemy line," David shouted to one of his captains. As he did so, he ducked a Philistine sword and lunged forward with lethal force, plunging his sword into his enemy. His captain turned away and began making his way north of David's position, shouting as he went, placing the men on notice that they would soon focus their energy at the heart of their enemy's position, hoping to divide their line.

The armies of Israel, led by David and Jonathan, the son of King Saul, were in the third day of a campaign just beyond the norther border of Israel against the Philistines. The goal of the conflict to drive Israel's enemy out of some of the unfortified cities that had fallen to the Philistines at the tail end of the priestly ministry of Eli. The two generals were confident that this effort would break the back of Philistine occupation.

As he continued to engage the enemy, David knew that his friend Jonathan was south of his position, himself engaged in hand to hand combat.

Their friendship was remarkable. Jonathan was aware that years earlier the prophet Samuel had anointed David to succeed Jonathan's father Saul as the king of Israel. Saul had often tried to use this fact to drive a wedge between the two men. Despite this, the prince remained as close a friend as one could have. Either man would willingly lay down his life for the other if the situation demanded.

Returning his focus to the battle at hand, David caught sight of the flash of a Philistine blade cutting through the air directly over his head. He had been careless. He quickly attempted to raise his sword to defend himself, but as he did, he realized his hand was empty. Ducking, he braced for the impact but felt none. For a moment he wondered if he was already dead.

His mind was confused. He felt cold and damp. Could this be what it was like, the moment after death?

Suddenly he took a deep, desperate breath and sat bolt upright. Opening his eyes he saw nothing. Still confused, he rubbed his face in an effort to brush off the fog of sleep. He had been dreaming. The familiar sound of dripping water helped the future king grab on to reality. He was in a cave.

David and those following him had found refuge in one of the caves within the stronghold of En Gedi, a wilderness oasis just west of the Salt Sea. He was on the run from King Saul who, realizing that his own sons would never rule over Israel as long as David lived, was hunting his former soldier. The diversion of Saul's attention towards David had now begun to bring harm on the nation. Now the Philistines were capturing territory that Israel had claimed at a high cost.

David pulled his legs up near his chest and looked around the dimly lit cave. He could see several of his men who had followed him in his flight from Saul. Behind him, deep in the cave, many more quietly slept. Many of these men were themselves fugitives from the king. Others had joined David realizing that the future of the nation was with this man. Together they formed a formidable fighting force.

He drew in a deep breath and stood, cautiously making his way over and around bodies toward the front of the cave. How had it come to this, running for his life and hiding in a cave? He thought back to the emotions that had filled his heart the day Samuel had anointed him to eventually succeed Saul as the king of Israel. He had hoped the king would remain ignorant of the events of that day, but somehow Saul had found out.

As David stepped over another sleeping man, his hand brushed against a leather pouch fastened at his side. He still carried it with him daily, the same pouch from which he had drawn the stone that had brought down the giant Goliath. From that great victory he had quickly risen to an almost legendary status in Israel. They had even sung songs about him. But that was years ago. It seemed like a lifetime ago. Now he had begun to wonder if he would ever get out of the wilderness.

As unexpected as were the giant moments that marked David's life years before, even so was the route that had led him to become a fugitive in the wilderness.

He stepped to the mouth of the cave and looked up from his position to where the cliffs of En Gedi met the sky. The sun would soon rise. It would certainly be another hot day, but at this time of the morning the air was cool and fresh. David looked straight ahead to a small waterfall that dropped into a pool directly beneath his position. As he followed the path of the water, his breath caught by what he saw.

He ducked behind a rock as his cousin Joab knelt quietly beside him, placing a hand on his shoulder. Beside the pool of water and stretching out in a broad circle were scores of sleeping men. Here and there among the men were what remained of campfires from the previous night. The noise of the waterfall must have concealed the noise of their arrival.

David remained motionless as he waited for more light to reveal the identity of their visitors. He figured it was highly probable that this was a detachment of Saul's men, sent to hunt him. Could it be that the king himself was among them?

As the light began to increase, he set his gaze on the center of the group of men. If the king was present, that is where he would have slept. He could clearly see a flag gently moving in the morning air, but could not make out the image. As he continued to focus on the flag, he began to make out the familiar crest of the king.

Joab squeezed David's shoulder, grabbed his hand and placed a sword in it. David knew what Joab had in mind. As he shifted his position, David noticed movement below in the camp. Someone in the center of the circle was moving. The figure rose and began his own dance to avoid waking those around him. The man was moving toward the path that would lead to the very cave in which David and his men were hiding. By his gait, David could tell it was the king.

David slipped back into the darkness of the cave with Joab close behind. They knelt behind the first corner and turned back toward the mouth of the cave. As they did, a few moments later the figure of Saul appeared, silhouetted against the dim morning light. They could see him clearly, though the light would not be sufficient to reveal to Saul the danger that lay just a few feet beyond the reach of the light.

As the king stepped toward the wall of the cave and prepared to relieve himself, Joab whispered in David's ear: "This is what we have been waiting for. God told you this day would come. You could be the king by nightfall."

David's grip on the sword tightened as he quietly rose and began to slowly make his way toward the king. He would send a message to all of Israel on this day.

Hidden by the darkness of the cave, he crept forward until he was just an arm's length from the king. His slow movements covered by the noise of the waterfall outside the mouth of the cave, David reached out with his sword and cut off a small portion of the king's robe.

The future king remained motionless as the current king finished his business and made his way toward the mouth of the cave. The message David hoped to communicate to the nation of Israel was that his heart toward the king was right. If he were to one day be king, it would not be by his doing. David would have no part in ending the reign of Saul.

Giant Moments

* 6 *

ON March 3, 1893, Amy Carmichael boarded the S.S. Valetta as it prepared to set out for Shanghai. Her ultimate destination would be the mission field of India. Originally from Ireland, she would serve for many years without furlough, primarily ministering to children who were trapped in what amounted to forced prostitution. More than five decades later she wrote of the day of her departure to the mission field expressing her feelings on that day: "Never, I think, not even in heaven shall I forget that parting. It was such a rending thing that I never wanted to repeat it...Even now my heart winces at the thought of it."[1]

Giant moments such as this mark our lives forever. They represent the crossing of a line behind which we can never again step.

A Day ~~Like~~ Unlike Any Other

Giant moments rarely announce themselves beforehand. They begin as a day no different than any other. The first giant moment we read about in David's life was a day that began as usual. He had set out to put the sheep to pasture with his staff in hand and shepherd's sling at his side. By the end of the day he had been marked as the heir *un*apparent to Saul's kingdom.

Saul, Israel's first king had been noteworthy because of his stature. He was said to have stood head and shoulders above all others in Israel. But of his spiritual life prior to his anointing, there was nothing noteworthy. In fact it was not until after he was anointed by the prophet that we learn anything of his heart. As Saul departed from Samuel following the anointing, we read that "God gave him another heart."[2]

As Samuel set out to find Saul's successor, the Lord made it clear that the only qualification He was looking for was one who possessed a heart that was already in the right place. This clarification was given by God because even the great prophet Samuel was caught up in looking first at the outward appearance of a man.

When he was sent by God to the home of Jesse of Bethlehem to anoint a new king, the impressive stature of Jesse's oldest son Eliab caused Samuel to say, "Surely the Lord's anointed is before Him!" His assessment prompted God to respond: "Do not look at his appearance or at his physical stature, because I have refused him."[3] God made it clear that He was seeking one who had the heart to be king.

As David's spiritual life took shape in the unimpressive sheepfold, the eyes of the Lord were running "to and fro throughout the whole earth" seeking one whose heart was loyal to Him.[4] After Samuel exhausted all the options presented by Jesse, David was called in from the pasture. As David stood before Samuel, the Lord said, "Arise, anoint him; for this is the one!"[5]

God had found His king. David had been faithful in the unimpressive place he had begun. Now he was set on an unpredictable route that would lead to the throne.

In geometry one learns that the shortest distance between two points is a straight line. It is, however, rare to find a straight line in life that can take you from point A to point B. David found out pretty quickly that it would not be a straight line from the sheepfold to the throne. In fact he would have to endure years of waiting before his calling would become a reality.

As the people of Israel followed Moses out from Egypt, we read: "Then it came to pass, when Pharaoh had let the people go, that God did not lead them by the way of the land of the Philistines, although that was near; for God said, 'Lest perhaps the people change their minds when they see war, and return to Egypt'" (Exodus 13:17). The shortest route from Egypt to the Promised Land was through the land controlled by the Philistines.

Someone has said, "The shortest route is not always the best route." God knew that the people were not prepared to take this route, so He "led the people around by the way of the wilderness of the Red Sea."[6] A trip that could have been completed in an estimated eleven days took forty years.

There were a couple factors that affected the "distance" between Egypt and the Promised Land. The first as noted was the wisdom of God in leading them around the territory held by the Philistines. The second factor was the response of the people.

Not long after leaving Egypt, the people of Israel did actually arrive at the border of the land promised to them by God. Moses sent a dozen men across the border to spy out the land. The majority returned with a report which discouraged the hearts of the people. Joshua and Caleb stood alone in their conviction that the inhabitants of the land could be defeated. The majority report was believed, and the people began talking of plans to return to Egypt.

These two factors, God's wisdom and man's response, always factor into the length of the route from our unimpressive beginning to our unexpected destination. In Philippians 2:12-13 we read: "Work out your own salvation with fear and trembling; for it is God who works in you both to will and to do for His good pleasure." The route is never independent of either God's leading or our response.

From the moment of the anointing, God had David on a route that would ultimately lead to the throne. It was not a straight line, but one that would take him from the heights of being a great champion in Israel to the depths of running for his life from King Saul. It would test his ability to trust the timing and process of God when the opportunity to take Saul out presented itself.

The Ultimate Giant Moment

David's ultimate giant moment began again like any other day and ended like no other. He had been sent by his father to check on the welfare of the three oldest boys in the family who were fighting with King Saul as Israel faced the Philistines, or so it was believed. The truth was the battle was at a stalemate following a challenge presented by a Philistine champion named Goliath. While Saul stood head and shoulders above all in Israel, Goliath was head and shoulders above Saul, checking in at over nine feet tall.

In 1 Samuel 17 David arrives on the scene just in time to hear the giant's defiant challenge: "Give me a man, that we may fight together" (vs 10). The young shepherd took the challenge personally and began to look for some answers. He asked, "What shall be done for the man who takes away the reproach from Israel?" (vs 26).

Whether out of a jealous spirit or the protective heart of an older brother, Eliab attempted to discourage David's inquiries, saying, "Why did you come down here? And with whom have you left those few sheep in the wilderness?" (vs 28). David's place was with the sheep. Their father had made that evident when Samuel the prophet had come for a visit. What was David hoping to accomplish? What did a shepherd know about warfare, much less fighting giants?

For David to deal with this giant he would first have to escape the shadow of the sheepfold. The shadow of the sheepfold is cast by our unimpressive beginnings. For some it may be the shadow cast by the drug addiction which held sway when Christ found them. For others the shadow might be a childhood diagnosis of a learning disability.

Our response to the things that overshadow our lives will affect the time and distance required to reach our unexpected destination.

While the sheepfold will be used by God for critical character development, it can also restrict our future progress. Consider what might have happened had David taken to heart the tone and words of his brother? He would have certainly lacked the courage to face the giant.

Let's take a moment to consider Joseph, the son of the Jewish patriarch Jacob, in the book of Genesis. As a young man his brothers derisively referred to him as "the dreamer." What if he would have taken the tone of their words to heart? Years later as he sat in the Egyptian prison listening to the dream of the butler and baker, would he have had the courage to trust God for the interpretation?

We must take care what we take to heart. The sheepfold may be what defines your identity at the beginning, but the wind of God's Spirit is going to blow in your life, and you will be moved beyond your unimpressive beginnings. What defined you at the beginning need not be what defines you at the end.

Perhaps even more difficult to escape than the way others define us, may be the struggle to escape the way we define ourselves. I think it is interesting to note that David felt his experience as a shepherd, rather than hindering his potential, made him the ideal candidate to take out the giant. Later in the narrative he told King Saul, "Your servant has killed both lion and bear; and this uncircumcised Philistine will be like one of them."[7]

There was no known career track that David could climb from the sheepfold to the throne. When one begins as a shepherd, it does not matter how hard you work, how many sheep you save or how large the flock grows, there is no ladder of promotion you can climb that will take you to the throne. From beginning to end his steps would have to be directed by God.

It is faith that released David from the shadow of the sheepfold into the call of God. Faith declared, "Nothing is impossible with God." With this in mind, why couldn't a shepherd kill a giant?

David's response to his oldest brother's derisive comments is noteworthy: "What have I done now? Is there not a cause?"[8] David clearly believed that he knew something of which Eliab was unaware. We next read, "Then he turned from him toward another and said the same thing."

We do not know what motivated Eliab. Whatever it was, to follow the Lord, David would have to turn away from discouraging counsel. To follow God there will be times when we may need to do the same.

In 1999, two good friends of mine, Joseph and Mandi, set out from their home in Zimbabwe, on a path that would eventually lead them to settle in America. The troubling economic situation in their homeland made the move seem like a simple decision.

The problem was as Joseph began to speak of their plans to friends and family, they immediately faced resistance. They were reminded of many others just like them who had been turned back during the emigration process. Why would they be any different?

Joseph explained their convictions to me: "Even though at the time it seemed folly to many that we should leave behind everything we knew and venture into uncertainty, we believed the Lord was with us." This was the same conviction that enabled David to press through negative counsel that could have turned him away from his course.

But how should we respond to counsel when it comes from a heart that is full of both faith and a genuine desire for our good? Proverbs tells us that there is safety in many counselors. Does this mean that good counsel is always right?

The Apostle Paul is an interesting case study in turning away from good counsel. In Acts 20 we find him in the city of Miletus. There he calls the leaders of the Ephesian church together. As they gather he tells them, "I go bound in the spirit to Jerusalem, not knowing the things that will happen to me there, except that the Holy Spirit testifies in every city, saying that chains and tribulation await me."[9]

Paul explained that he had resolved himself to traveling to Jerusalem, though the Counselor, the Holy Spirit, had revealed that trouble awaited him there. The trouble which awaited the Apostle in Jerusalem is revealed again just a few verses later in another city.

We are told of a prophet named Agabus who traveled from Judea to warn Paul of the trouble that awaited him in Jerusalem.[10]

Despite all the warnings of trouble ahead, we read in Acts 21:15, "After those days we packed and went up to Jerusalem." There certainly is no Counselor more reliable than the Holy Spirit, and yet Paul chose to proceed with his planned trip to Jerusalem.

Counsel that seems to discourage us from our planned course will serve a couple purposes. First, it may come as a test of our resolve in following the course which God has set for us. Has God called you to a difficult task? If you cannot press through contrary advice, you will never make it through the struggles that lie between you and the completion of your task. Secondly, I believe that God may allow discouraging counsel to arise so that when difficulty is faced we will know that we were warned.

I recall some time ago counseling a Christian business man against a decision he was considering. I could foresee several potential pitfalls in the proposition, which I hoped to help him avoid. Ultimately he went ahead with his plans, despite my counsel and his experience in the endeavor was as I suggested it might be.

Did he make a mistake in rejecting the advice I gave him? I don't believe he did, but I do believe that God wanted him aware of the challenges that may be ahead.

In Luke 14:27 Jesus says, "Whoever does not bear his cross and come after Me cannot be My disciple." He proceeds to encourage people to count the cost of discipleship. If you did not know better, it would seem that He was discouraging people from being His follower. What He is in fact doing is letting His listeners know that there is a very real cost to being a disciple. If you have chosen to follow Jesus, do not be surprised that there is a cross to bear.

Who's the Underdog?

Whenever a sporting event features a prohibitive favorite, you can be sure that the David vs. Goliath analogy will be thrown around. I call to mind the talk leading up to the 2007 Super Bowl featuring the undefeated New England Patriots and the New York Giants. The Giants had snuck into the playoffs as the Wild Card contender; while the Patriots were on the verge of completing a historic run of perfection. I recall one pregame commentator saying that even if the Giants won the Super Bowl, the Patriots would still be considered the greatest team in NFL history. But did the David vs. Goliath analogy fit?

Following the Giants victory, the outcome of the game was being described as one of the biggest upsets in American sports history. What may not be remembered is that on the final weekend of that regular season, as the Patriots were pressing to finish undefeated, the Giants nearly beat New England. Perhaps the outcome of that Super Bowl was not, in reality, that great of an upset.

If we look beyond the headlines of David's battle with Goliath, we may find that even this outcome was perhaps not the upset it may have seemed. Was it possible that David held the advantage against Goliath?

Our information about the giant is found in 1 Samuel 17:4-7. We are told that his height was "six cubits and a span." With a cubit being approximately eighteen inches and a span about half that, the estimate is that Goliath stood about 9'9" tall. Reading on we learn:

> "He had a bronze helmet on his head, and he was armed with a coat of mail, and the weight of the coat was five

thousand shekels of bronze. And he had bronze armor on his legs and a bronze javelin between his shoulders. Now the staff of his spear was like a weaver's beam, and his iron spearhead weighed six hundred shekels; and a shield bearer went before him."

Let's first consider the giant's apparel. This was long before helmets came into use that had protection for the face. While Goliath's head was protected by his bronze helmet, his face was exposed to David. He wore a protective coat of mail that weighed approximately 125 pounds. Add to that the weight of his bronze leg armor, and it would be easy to conclude that agility would not have been one of the giant's advantages. David would be relatively safe if he maintained some distance between himself and the bulky giant.

In terms of weaponry, Goliath would have been very imposing. He carried a bronze javelin which apparently remained sheathed throughout the battle. His weapon of choice for this encounter was his spear which is described as similar to a weaver's beam with a 600 shekel iron spearhead. To make it convenient for carrying, it would likely have been nearly as tall as the giant. Imagine an eight foot 2x2 with a fifteen-pound iron spearhead at the end. This weapon would have been deadly at close range, but from a distance it would not have posed a serious threat. The size of the spearhead would require an exceptionally heavy staff to provide proper balancing. Even then the strongest man would have struggled to throw such a spear with any accuracy.

Across the field stood the young shepherd with nothing but a staff, a sling and five stones. As for his apparel, when King Saul offered David his armor, he had declined, fearing it would make him clumsy. What David knew was that he would probably have no need for the armor. He had no intention of getting close enough to the giant to allow his weapons to pose any real threat.

In regards to David's weaponry, a sling and a stone seem like a paltry arsenal by comparison to that of Goliath. Yet when we consider ancient warfare, we find that assumption may be flawed.

The Greek historian Xenophon wrote of his experiences as a soldier during the 4th and 5th centuries B.C. in *Anabasis*. Here he notes that slingers had a greater range than "javelin men."[11] In addition, Xenophon noted that as a leader of an army of Greek mercenaries, it was imperative that they "get slingers as soon as possible."[12]

As we look to the biblical record we find that within the tribe of Benjamin there were seven hundred left-handed warriors who "could sling a stone at a hair's breadth and not miss."[13] Elsewhere we read of men who would later follow David who could use either the left or right hand to accurately hurl a stone.[14]

In looking at the match-up with fresh eyes, we find Goliath who was imposing in his size and immense in his strength, yet lacking in both agility and long-range weaponry. Across the field is the agile young shepherd who has shown himself to be an expert at slinging stones. David's weapon, a sling, had a greater effective range than Goliath's best weapon, the javelin. Who are you going to take in the battle? Former *Revivaltime* radio host, Pastor Dan Betzer once commented that David was the only one on the battlefield who knew the giant did not stand a chance.

As we are aware, David was victorious in his legendary battle against the giant. In 1 Samuel 17:48-50 we read:

> "So it was, when the Philistine arose and came and drew near to meet David, that David hurried and ran toward the

army to meet the Philistine. Then David put his hand in his bag and took out a stone; and he slung it and struck the Philistine in his forehead, so that the stone sank into his forehead, and he fell on his face to the earth. So David prevailed over the Philistine with a sling and a stone, and struck the Philistine and killed him."

Keys to Victory

There were several keys to David's victory. The first was in terms of his strategy. He had no intention of wrestling the giant. Had he allowed Goliath to get too close, the advantage would have swung to his opponent. But if he could maintain some distance for his sling to remain effective, he knew that he could defeat the Philistine.

In reality, there were probably many among the ranks of Saul's army who, with the same arsenal, could have easily defeated Goliath. David was certainly not the only crack shot with a sling on the side of Israel. What set David apart was the second key to victory, that being faith. He believed that the giant could be defeated.

When facing an opponent or an obstacle the size of Goliath, there are two options: fear or faith. Fear paralyzes, while faith emboldens. Saul's soldiers were paralyzed at the sight of Goliath. In 1 Samuel 17:24 we read that when the men of Israel saw the giant, they all "fled from him and were dreadfully afraid." Yet when David faced the giant, he ran toward him.[15] Faith was the difference maker for David.

Evangelist Leonard Ravenhill once described faith, saying, "Faith reckons, risks and rests." The word "reckon" is an accounting term. It suggests that we do a little math. When David did the math he concluded that he could defeat the giant.

Within the mathematical equation David used, we find his third key to victory. Although he may have had the skill to defeat Goliath, he included God in the equation. David said, "The Lord will deliver you into my hand...for the battle is the Lord's."[16] Saul's soldiers reckoned that none of them had the ability to defeat Goliath. David reckoned that with God he could bring the giant down, and he did.

Abraham did a little math of his own when called by God to offer his son Isaac as a sacrifice in Genesis 22. Was it blind obedience that moved Abraham to bind his son to the altar? Hardly. Scripture tells us in Hebrews 11:19 that a part of his consideration was his "Accounting that God was able to raise (Isaac) up, even from the dead."[17] Within Abraham's mathematical equation was a consideration of God's ability and the promise God had made concerning Isaac's descendants. Faith gave him the courage to obey.

After reckoning, David risked. He stepped out to face Goliath. Were there any guarantees of victory? Hebrews 11 tells us of men and women of faith, some of whom "became valiant in battle," while others "had trial(s) of mockings and scourgings, yes, and of chains and imprisonment."[18] No, there was no guarantee of a victorious outcome. Risk is an inescapable element of faith. At the same time we have found that apart from faith we cannot please God. The conclusion is that you cannot follow God without the reality of risk.

I experienced this first hand when my wife Jen and I worked toward purchasing a different house in 2013. As we progressed through the process, my hobby became crunching numbers in an attempt to determine if we would be able to afford the home we were considering. I would find $40 here or $55 there that we could save by making some changes. Every time we would go out to eat

I would scribble on napkins our expected cash flow. I was trying to find a way to make the purchase as low risk as possible.

This is certainly a good practice, after all, Jesus told us to count the cost. At the end of the day, however, I realized that no matter how often I crunched the numbers, making the purchase would require that we would step out in faith and take a risk.

Without question, rest is the most difficult of the three R's of faith. We reckon, we risk and rather than rest, we often look for an escape route. It was not long after following Moses out of Egypt that Israel began looking for a path of retreat. Why? Because they began to face some stiff opposition and obstacles. When they should have been resting, they were scheming.

This is a very real temptation for us. We start out in faith, have a few doors close in our face and what do we do? We want to turn around. Or we start grumbling and complaining, looking for those who will sympathize with our plight. What would God have us do? Rest! Don't move, just rest.

The danger in looking back is that we may well get stuck. In Genesis 19 we read of the destruction of Sodom and Gomorrah. Having been rescued by a pair of angels from the destruction sent from God, Lot and his family fled for their lives. But as they moved further from what they had always known, the temptation to look back became overwhelming. The text tells us, "Lot's wife looked back behind them, and she became a pillar of salt" (Gen 19:26).

A similar fate may befall us in our walk of faith. As soon as we look back, we run the risk of getting stuck in place. You have reckoned and risked, now rest. Keep moving forward, resting in the conclusion of your faith. Until one reaches this place, the temptation to retreat will never subside.

Have you ever noticed the strange phenomenon that no matter how bad things were in the past, we tend to most clearly remember the good? Equally strange is the belief that things were always better in the past.

The people of Israel demonstrated this clearly. Though Egypt was for them a place of slavery, they continually sought to return rather than rest. In fact a number of them did return to Egypt during the prophetic ministry of Jeremiah.[19] They looked to this route despite the fact that God had clearly warned the people that Egypt was not the answer.

Retreat from the conclusions of faith is never the answer. God's instruction to us is the same as it was to Israel through the prophet Isaiah: "In returning and rest you shall be saved; in quietness and confidence shall be your strength" (Isaiah 30:15). We think the answer is to turn back from the route we are on. We figure we must have made a mistake when we reckoned that with God we could do it. God says, "No, the answer is to return to the path of faith and rest. There you shall be saved and find strength." Will you retreat or rest?

Rest is the most difficult part of faith because obstacles will always come, and will not always move out of the way quickly. What we do at that point will determine the eventual outcome. Remember, spirit produces spirit while flesh produces flesh. To retreat is to turn to the flesh, ensuring fleshly results. To rest in faith is to continue in the Spirit and to ensure the continued effect of the wind principle.

If You Will Believe

As I have thought about David's conquest over the giant, I have often thought it interesting that God received glory for an outcome that was not necessarily miraculous. As we have noted, with

David's arsenal and the proper strategy, he would certainly have been the favorite against Goliath. How then is it that God continues to receive glory for the outcome?

The answer can be found in the story of Lazarus in the eleventh chapter of John's Gospel. You may be familiar with the story, but allow me to give a short review.

Lazarus was one of Jesus' best friends. The Lord had often spent time at the home in Bethany which Lazarus shared with his sisters, Mary and Martha. One day word came from these women that their brother was sick. They were hoping that Jesus would travel to Bethany in time to heal their brother. By the time Jesus did arrive on the scene, Lazarus had already been dead and in the tomb for four days. As we discovered previously, Jesus has often been known to turn a funeral into a celebration. By the end of that day Lazarus was no longer dead, having been called out of the tomb by Jesus.

The key verse for our purposes is found in John 11:40. Martha is understandably concerned about the outcome of the situation. In this passage, Jesus reminds her, "Did I not say to you that if you would believe you would see the glory of God?"

Why does God continue to receive glory for David's victory over the giant even though the outcome may not necessarily have been a miracle? The reason is because David believed in and depended on God.

The two giant moments that have marked my life the most over the past decade both involve my kids. The first was what transpired in the year following the birth of our daughter Malley. As I mentioned previously, a congenital liver condition led to her placement on the organ donor recipient list.

During those months I would often take her with me to our church in the evening to pray that God would heal her. I knew that a transplant would likely have a good outcome, but I would reason in prayer that if the doctors did the work, they would receive the glory. I would seek God in prayer that He would intervene and take the glory for the outcome. I went so far in prayer as to promise that if God would heal her by His hand, apart from a transplant, I would go to every home in our community to tell about it.

A month after her first birthday we got the call that an organ was available. Doctors at the University of Minnesota Amplatz Children's Hospital performed the successful transplant, and her health began to noticeably improve within a week. We were very grateful for the way things progressed, but I continued to struggle with the thought that only the doctors would receive the glory since they did the work.

I saw an opportunity to give God glory a month later when a local news station called asking for the opportunity to do a story about her for the evening news. As they sat in our small living room with a camera to hear our story, we frequently repeated the ways in which we had found help and hope through the Bible.

My thoughts were that this would be the final opportunity for God to receive glory for what had happened in the life of our daughter. The next evening I was discouraged to watch the report, as it made no mention of our relationship with Christ or the ways that faith in God had helped us endure a very difficult season.

I think that at the heart of my struggle was the feeling that despite our prayer, so much had progressed just the way that the doctors had predicted. She did need corrective surgery, and it did not fix the problem; she did quit eating, and she did need the transplant. Where was the hand of God in the process? All had transpired just as we were told to expect.

And yet something did happen that I never expected. We repeatedly heard people giving God praise for the outcome. They talked of how He had answered our prayers. "What a miracle!" was a common refrain. In my heart I wondered, how is it that God is receiving glory for a work the doctors had accomplished?

I think that the answer lies in Christ's words to Martha: "Did I not say to you that if you would believe you would see the glory of God?" This explains why God continues to receive the glory for the outcome of David's battle with Goliath. If you will believe, God will receive glory, even if the outcome is not necessarily miraculous.

We tend to believe that what is needed for God to receive glory is a miracle. How many of us have said, "If only God would perform a miracle in this situation, imagine how many people would believe in Him"? While it may seem that more miracles would mean more glory for God, and thus more conversions, the Bible makes it clear that this is not necessarily the case.

Recall the story of the Rich Man and Lazarus (a different Lazarus) in Luke 16:19-31. In the story both men die and enter eternity. Scripture reveals that the rich man went into torment while Lazarus entered Paradise.

What we find is that the rich man is able to see Lazarus in Paradise standing alongside the Old Testament patriarch Abraham. He calls out asking that Lazarus be sent back to warn his family "lest they also come to this awful place." Abraham explains that the living have the law and the prophets to warn them. The rich man responds, "No, father Abraham; but if one goes to them from the dead, they will repent." Abraham responds, "If they do not hear Moses and the prophets, neither will they be persuaded though one rise from the dead."

What a staggering indictment of our society. One *has* returned from the dead, and most pay no attention. Jesus Himself said, "I am He who lives, and was dead, and behold, I am alive forevermore."[20] The problem is not a lack of miracles, but an issue in the heart of man. People refuse to believe the testimony that has already been given. So no, more miracles would not necessarily equate to more people placing faith in Christ. Miracles may impress the nonbeliever, but they will not necessarily evoke a response of committed faith.

I would like to look back to a previous illustration surrounding the martyrdom of the apostles. We understand from tradition and early writers that nearly all of them were executed for their testimony of Christ. What would have been the effect if Jesus Himself had come to earth to rescue each of these men from their fate? There would have certainly been incredible glory that God would have received at that time, but what effect would it have on us today?

Because God did *not* rescue them, we are provided with proof that these first-hand witnesses of Jesus were convinced of His identity, to the point that they were willing to die for their belief. Because God did *not* rescue them, He continues to receive glory, much more so than He would have received had He provided them with an avenue of escape.

The reality is that there is glory that God receives when a believer remains unmoved through trials that is every bit as potent as the glory He receives through miraculous deliverances. Do not despise your non-miraculous giant moments. You never know the lasting glory God may take for Himself through such experiences. Continue to believe and you *will* see the glory of God.

Wishing Yourself into Extinction

What is it that gives an individual a unique identity? For our purposes, we will identify two factors: biological and experiential. Your unique biological makeup and your experiences work together to make you who you are. If either of these factors were different, you would be an entirely different person.

This fact struck me several days after the birth of our fourth child, Silas James. Several months prior to his birth, following an ultrasound, our doctor told us that he had identified several things that suggested the possibility of a genetic disorder. Further testing confirmed his suspicions.

Silas was born a week before his due date, weighing barely half as much as his older siblings at the time of their birth. He lived for only a day and a half, before passing into eternity.

The condition which took his life was Trisomy-18, a condition which resulted in an extra chromosome in the 18th set of every cell within his body. This genetic foul-up cost him his life. At the same time, it was that very genetic information within his body that made him a unique individual.

If we could have somehow gone back to remove the extra chromosome in his genetic makeup, the result would have been a different person. He would have had the same name, but would not have been the same child. So would we have wanted a different son? Certainly not. What we wanted was a son free of the symptoms that accompanied his genetic make-up.

Similarly, our circumstances work together to form a sort of genetic make-up that gives us our unique identity. Looking back to Psalm 139, David writes, "In Your book they all were written, the days fashioned for me, when as yet there were none of them."

What happens if you significantly change the material within the pages of a book? You have a different story. To wish away your painful experiences, would be to wish away yourself.

In the book *Why Suffering?*, coauthored by Vince Vitale and Ravi Zacharias, Vitale says this: "We think we wish God had allowed a different sort of world to exist, but in doing so we unwittingly wish ourselves, and those we love, out of existence."[21]

It seems logical that a world with no possibility of suffering would be preferable to the world we know. But as we dig into the nature of what is possible because of suffering, we find an entirely different perspective. Vitale continues: "Without the possibility of suffering, practically every great true story of history would be false. No one would ever have made a significant sacrifice for anyone else. No great moments of forgiveness and reconciliation. No opportunities to stand for justice against injustice."

He concludes his thought asking if it is really so obvious that a world without the possibility of suffering would be better. "We fail to recognize," says Vitale, "how much good would be lost in losing the possibility of the bad."[22]

If you research Trisomy-18, you will find that there are a number of common effects which accompany the condition which have a devastating impact on an unborn child's development. I recall praying that rather than necessarily seeing his genetic make-up altered, that God would work in such a way that none of the effects of the extra chromosome would touch our son's life.

Similarly, painful experiences have common effects on an individual. They often result in bitterness, fear, hatred and the like. These effects can devastate your life. Rather than wasting your time wishing away pain, determine through God that you will overcome the effects of such experiences. Choose to live in forgiveness. Face your failures and try again. Recognize that by

His blood, Christ has purchased those painful experiences and intends to redeem them for some good purpose.[23]

Wilderness University

To this point, David had seemingly lived a charmed life. He was anointed as the successor to King Saul and had become a national hero when he defeated the Philistine giant Goliath. But as unexpected as were those events, equally so was that which was in his immediate future.

In 1 Samuel 18:7, we find it recorded that as the people came to greet the army of Saul following a victory over the Philistines, the women sang, "Saul has slain his thousands, and David his ten thousands." The songs which sang of the glory to which David had risen would serve to be the thing which prompted his fall from grace. King Saul began to see his heroic warrior as a threat to his kingdom, and a verse later we read, "So Saul eyed David from that day forward."

Saul's insecurities took root within him to such a degree that he would make multiple attempts on David's life. Eventually we read, "Then David arose and fled that day from before Saul."[1] This event marked the beginning of years of living in the wilderness on the run from Israel's king. In his book, *The Making of a Man of God*, Alan Redpath writes:

> "Here was David, chosen to be king, destined to be master over great lands and wealth, but living in exile and begging bread. Anointed by the Spirit of God was David, but running for his life from his enemies and destitute of all his friends. So often the providences of God seem to run completely counter to His promises, but only that He may test our faith, only that He may ultimately accomplish His purpose for our lives in a way that He could never do if the path were always smooth. It is when problems and difficulties seem to be overwhelming that the man of God learns some lessons that he could never learn otherwise."[2]

The years David spent in the wilderness made him a part of Wilderness University, one of the most prestigious institutions of learning in history, at least in terms of its alumni list. The Apostle Paul was enrolled for three years prior to his emergence as a leader within the early church. Joseph was a student during the thirteen years he lived in Egypt as a slave and a prisoner. Moses put all other alumni to shame by his forty year enrollment.

Headlining the Wilderness University alumni list is one whom we would assume would never need the lessons that are taught by such seasons. But as with every other enrollee, it was here that he learned things that He could never have otherwise learned.

In Luke 4:1 we read, "Then Jesus, being filled with the Holy Spirit, returned from the Jordan and was led by the Spirit into the wilderness." The first thing noteworthy is that the same Spirit moving you and me from our insignificant beginnings toward our unexpected destination is the One who led Jesus into the wilderness of temptation. What purpose could such an experience serve to the Son of God? Certainly He had no need of such lessons as those taught by problems and difficulties. Or did He?

In the book of Hebrews, we read two passages that provide an answer to that question. The first comes in Hebrews 2:10 where we read that God intended to "make the captain of (our) salvation perfect through sufferings." We find a similar reference a few chapters later in Hebrews 5:8-9, as we read, "Though He was a Son, yet He learned obedience by the things which He suffered. And having been perfected, He became the author of eternal salvation to all who obey Him."

This seems to contradict our understanding of the Son of God. Wasn't He eternally perfect? In what way could He possibly need to be made perfect?

This passage brings together two words which regularly go together in our experience: obedience and suffering. Obedience to the Gospel has caused many to suffer throughout history. We too will likely suffer in some way as we strive to remain spotless in this world. Now consider this: We can be fairly certain that before coming to earth in the form of man, the Son's obedience to the Father never resulted in suffering. He did not know what it was like to suffer for doing right. We will look into this more in a moment.

Looking through the book of Hebrews, we find a theme emerging. It is this, that in Christ, God has established something better. The book teaches of a better hope (7:19), a better covenant (7:22), better promises (8:6), and better sacrifices (9:23). In accomplishing this God would make available a better possession (10:34), a better country (11:16), and a better resurrection (11:35).

Included in that which God sought to improve upon through Christ was the high priestly ministry. The earthly high priest had one major thing going for him in that he could easily sympathize with those who went astray because he was subject to the same.[3] At the same time, this was also the great shortcoming of the earthly high priest. Just like those he represented, the high priest was a sinner who had fallen short of the glory of God. As a result he needed to offer sacrifices for his own sins as well as for those of the people.

In that respect, Christ immediately remedied the major shortcoming in the earthly high priest. Because He never sinned, He never needed to offer sacrifices for Himself.

But what of the positive attribute the earthly high priest brought to the table, that he was able to have compassion on those going astray? Was Jesus able to associate with us in our weakness? This is what made suffering a necessary part of Jesus' experience. Apart from suffering He would never have been able to sympathize with our experience. In that respect He would have fallen short of what was provided by the earthly high priest.

Suffering perfected Him in the role to which God had called Him. Suffering made Him the perfect High Priest. Thus we read in Hebrews 4:15, "We do not have a High Priest who cannot sympathize with our weaknesses, but was in all points tempted as we are, yet without sin."

If it was necessary that the captain of our salvation suffer, is it possible that we will escape some level of the same? It seems unlikely. Notice what is found in what I believe could be described as the model of Christian maturity in Philippians 3:7-11:

"But what things were gain to me, these I have counted loss for Christ. Yet indeed I also count all things loss for the excellence of the knowledge of Christ Jesus my Lord, for whom I have *suffered* the loss of all things, and count them as rubbish, that I may gain Christ and be found in Him, not having my own righteousness, which is from the law, but that which is through faith in Christ, the righteousness which is of God by faith; that I may know Him and the power of His resurrection, and the fellowship of His *suffering*, being conformed to His death, if, by any means, I may attain to the resurrection from the dead."

If there is a lesson in this, it is that we can expect an experience similar to that of Christ. I suspect you are like me in that you probably do not have a strong desire to share too much in the suffering of Christ. Even so, it is at least a comfort to know that the experience of suffering, which we all share, exists at the core of the Christian experience. We can take comfort in knowing that nothing strange is happening to us.[4]

What does it look like when we share in the suffering of Christ? To answer we need to identify what Christ's sufferings were like. In the wilderness He suffered through a prolonged season of fasting, refusing relief until it was provided by the Father. In the Garden of Gethsemane, He asked if possible, that the cup of suffering be removed from Him. On the cross He suffered unjustly.

When suffering in the wilderness through the fast, He experienced delay. When suffering in the garden, He experienced unanswered prayer.[5] When suffering unjustly on the cross, He experienced abandonment.[6]

By these measures, we could conclude that when we experience delay or prayers that seemingly go unanswered or the sting of injustice or the feeling of abandonment, we are in those moments sharing in the sufferings of Christ.

Clearly, few of us experience the same degree of suffering as did the Lord or the early disciples. So how is it that we could consider our 21st century First World problems to qualify as sharing in the suffering of Christ?

Recall for a moment what was said by one of the thieves crucified alongside Jesus. He commented to the other crucified thief that their condemnation was justified: "For we receive the due reward of our deeds."[7] He was hinting at something noteworthy. That being that suffering is easier to manage and accept when it is deserved. Additionally, there is a degree to which suffering can be easier to stomach when there is no hope of escape.

Is it not true that our suffering is compounded when God, who is able to deliver us out of any situation, delays His response? When the disciples fought to maintain control of their boat on the stormy sea of Galilee, not only did they have the storm to contend with, they also had to contend with the question that arose within their own hearts as Jesus slept in the rear of the boat: "Teacher, do You not care that we are perishing?"[8] And Jesus, as He was dying on the cross, not only had to suffer the agony of the crucifixion; He also suffered as He sought to answer the equally agonizing question, "My Father, why have you forsaken me?"[9]

Think for a moment of the counsel that Job's wife gave him in the midst of his suffering: "Curse God and die."[10] Why would she seemingly place the blame on God? Because God could have prevented Job's suffering or rescued him out of it, and yet to that point He had done neither. Job rejected her advice, and over the following three dozen chapters, his suffering was compounded by unanswered questions; 131 of them to be exact. These questions would have been moot had he followed her advice.

It is important to note the nature of the unanswered questions with which we may struggle. While Job certainly struggled to find an answer for what he was facing, one thing is certain, he knew there was an answer. Drawing from G.K. Chesterton, Ravi Zacharias has stated that for the Christian, "the fundamental questions are answered, the peripheral ones are relatively unanswered."[11]

We may not know why, but we know that God knows why. When we are in the midst of pain, we may or may not find that to be sufficient consolation. But it certainly leaves us in a far better place than the skeptic, for whom Zacharias says, the fundamental questions of life are left unanswered.[12] Not only do they lack an answer to the difficult questions of life, they also lack a hope of ever finding an answer. For the unbeliever, the question, "Why?" is a meaningless question.

Make no mistake, when you struggle through pain and difficulty, and remain faithful to the Lord, you are sharing in the sufferings of Christ. Through the delays and difficult questions and prayers that may seemingly go unanswered you are experiencing the same thing He experienced. Isn't it interesting that because He suffered, He can associate with our experience and when we suffer, we share in His experience?

God's Will in the Wilderness

IN John 6:28 the people ask Jesus a very practical question: "What shall we do, that we may work the works of God?" I am sure they assumed He would answer, "Love your neighbor" or "Give to the poor." What He explained, however, was that there was something much more foundational to the works that God expected. "This is the work of God," He answered, "That you believe in Him whom He sent." In looking to what they may have thought would be the will of God, they risked missing that which was most critical.

When we find ourselves in the wilderness, there is one overwhelming desire. That is, to get out. Now. We pray for an escape. We seek counsel. We declare that it is God's will that we get out. But in doing so, we risk missing something foundational to God's will as we experience the various wilderness moments of life. The Apostle Paul reveals it to us: "In everything give thanks; for this is the will of God in Christ Jesus for you."[1]

Let's turn our attention back to Jesus in the Garden of Gethsemane on the night He was arrested. There He prays, "Oh

My Father, if it is possible, let this cup pass from Me; nevertheless, not as I will, but as You will."[2]

But now go back in time just a few hours in the story. Jesus is sharing the Passover supper with His disciples. He is fully aware of what lies around the corner. We pick up the story as He institutes the Lord's Supper:

> "And as they were eating, Jesus took bread, blessed and broke it, and gave it to the disciples and said, 'Take, eat; this is My body.' Then He took the cup, and gave thanks…"[3]

Did you notice that? The cup He would later ask that the Father release Him from, He is here giving thanks for. He is expressing thanks for the cup that held all the sin of the world. In doing so, Jesus set for us an example of giving thanks in everything. Before He ever asked for the escape, He first gave thanks.

God's will for you in every situation is first that you give thanks; it is not first that you get out.

The reason we struggle to follow God's will in this point is because the perspective that brings thanksgiving in all situations often comes too late. The perspective that brings such a thankful heart often only comes through something we have lost.

Think back for a moment to another man who held a cup. This cup held stew and was in the hand of Esau, the grandson of Abraham. Esau had just returned from hunting and was famished. Happening upon his brother Jacob, he asked for a cup of the stew Jacob had prepared. Ever the opportunist, Jacob responded, "Sell me your birthright as of this day."[4]

Esau's reasoning went along this line: "I am going to die of hunger anyway. If I'm dead, what will this birthright do for me?" So he traded away what was most valuable for a moment of satisfaction. He had no perspective of what lie ahead. He overemphasized the moment at the expense of the future. Scripture tells us, "Thus Esau despised his birthright."[5]

Now fast forward to some point later in Esau's life. In the New Testament, we gain some insight on how Esau would later feel about this trade. In Hebrews 12:16-17, we are told of Esau, "Who for one morsel of food sold his birthright. For you know that afterward, when he wanted to inherit a blessing, he was rejected, for he found no place of repentance, though he sought it diligently with tears."

Listen carefully: There are some things that even repentance cannot recapture. No volume of tears could bring the birthright back to Esau. No amount of sorrow could recapture what had been lost. I wonder what went through Esau's mind after experience brought perspective. I wonder if he regretted that he had not been more thankful for his birthright, in spite of his hunger.

In August of 2013, Jen and I learned that we were expecting our fourth child, all of whom would be separated in age by nineteen months. Admittedly I was not thankful to be adding a fourth child to the mix, already having three kids age four and under.

In November of that year, an ultrasound revealed that our fourth child would also be our third son. I had hoped this child would be a girl, so rather than giving thanks, I was disappointed.

This child, born March 16, 2014, was our son Silas. As I mentioned previously, he lived only a day and a half due to a genetic disorder. My point is not to suggest that my failure to give thanks may have somehow contributed to the outcome. I know it did not. My point is that perspective has taught me that I should have been thankful at the news of this coming son.

I lost something in that experience that no amount of tears or even repentance could ever recapture; the chance to give thanks. Perspective has taught me that I should always give thanks, in every situation. You never know what God is up to, so be thankful.

But there is something else that we miss out on when we fail to give thanks. Consider this reality. When you are in high school you can't wait for college. When you are in college you can't wait to get out into the world. When you get out into the world you wish you could move back in with your mom. When you are single you wish you were married. When you are married you wish you had kids. When you have kids you wish they would grow up and move out. And it goes on.

What is the effect? We miss out on life constantly hoping for the next stage or wishing we could return to the good old days. Then when we are old we wish we could go back and get out of life what we missed. What is the answer? We must determine that we will be thankful, wherever we are.

The Apostle Paul explained: "Godliness with contentment is great gain."[6] How do we begin to live in the moment and enjoy today? It is not a different situation which is needed, but a change in perception. Do you want to change your life? If so, then choose to be thankful.

The importance of a thankful heart to our spiritual well-being cannot be overstated. In Luke 17 we find the story of Jesus healing and cleansing ten lepers. There we read:

"When (Jesus) saw them, He said to them, 'Go, show yourselves to the priests.' And so it was as they went, they were cleansed. And one of them, when he saw that he was healed, returned, and with a loud voice glorified God, and fell down on his face at His feet, and gave thanks." [7]

All ten of these men had faith enough to be healed. That is an important point. When Jesus sent them to show themselves to the priests, all ten immediately responded, though none of them had yet received healing. It was while they went that they were set free. Of the ten, only one had faith enough to return and give thanks. To him Jesus said, "Arise, go your way. Your faith has made you well." [8] The King James Version of the Bible reads, "Thy faith hath made thee whole."

Ten lepers were healed that day, but only one of the ten is described by Jesus as having been made "whole" or "well". The other nine, though well physically, lacked something in their faith. That something was a thankful heart. Because of this the other nine were healed, but not whole.

Let's take a look back at Esau. In Genesis 25:34 we find that in selling his birthright for a cup of soup, "Esau despised his birthright." He despised it for the sake of the moment. Why was it that Esau was willing to trade away his future for the moment? He lacked perspective.

But now backtrack a bit to the second verse in Hebrews 12. There we are instructed to look to Jesus, "Who for the joy that was set before Him endured the cross, despising the shame, and has sat down at the right hand of the throne of God." Whereas Esau considered the blessing of the future as nothing for the sake of the moment, Jesus considered as nothing the pain of the moment for the blessing of the future. He saw the joy set before Him, so He endured the cross.

If you are currently enrolled in Wilderness University, perspective is the key to your survival. You must see beyond the present discomfort to what lies beyond or you may be tempted like Esau to sell your future for the sake of the moment.

Sow Your Seed

Imagine the way a letter home from Wilderness University may read:

Dear Family,

I hope that you are well. Little has changed for me. Things are dry and discouraging. The way I felt when I set out is a distant memory. I have heard nothing to suggest how many more semesters I will endure until graduation.

I am at a point at which I am unsure what to do next. I hope that you can come visit me soon.

With love,

Your Son.

Recently I have spent a great deal of time visiting our local county jail. As I visit with inmates I emphasize to them that they can set a new course for their future by the decisions they make from that day forward.

Our decisions today are seeds that will produce a harvest, either to our good or harm, in the future. Listen to the advice of Solomon:

> "As you do not know what is the way of the wind, or how the bones grow in the womb of her who is with child, so you do not know the works of God who makes everything. In the morning sow your seed, and in the evening do not withhold your hand; for you do not know which will prosper, either this or that, or whether both alike will be good."[9]

I recall some time ago visiting with a friend who had just learned that he was facing some legal trouble stemming from decisions he had made years earlier. He had since committed his life to Christ, but now faced a situation that could possibly lead to prison time. I shared with him something I had come across in the Bible that I felt may hold some wisdom for his situation: "Blessed are you who sow beside all waters."[10]

Rather than sitting around seeing what might come of the situation, he began working every possible angle to see if he could get the charges dropped. In the end that is just what happened. God worked and he escaped a significant wilderness experience.

If you are in the wilderness, begin planting the seed today that will get you to the destination you hope to reach. Why get started today? Because God's good plans are tied to the seeds you sow. You never know, today might be the day you leave the wilderness.

We err if we wait for ideal conditions to begin planting our seed. We think, "Nothing will be produced in this wilderness." So we sit around waiting for better circumstances to come our way.

Here is a critical truth: ideal conditions will never come. Looking back to Solomon, we read, "He who observes the wind will not sow, and he who regards the clouds will not reap."[11] If you are looking for a reason to wait, you will always find one.

In 1 Corinthians 16:9 Paul explains, "A great and effective door has been opened to me, and there are many adversaries." The two go hand in hand: adversity and opportunity. This was true for Nehemiah as he sought to lead the rebuilding of the walls of Jerusalem. He was opposed at every turn by those who did not want to see Jerusalem rebuilt. As someone once said, "Whenever you find somebody who says for the sake of God, 'Let us arise and build,' I will guarantee you, you will always have someone who will say, 'Let us stand and tear down.'"

If you wait for ideal conditions, you will never get out of the wilderness. Begin sowing your seed. You never know, today may be your day.

Fruit In and Out of Season

In the first Psalm, we read a familiar passage which speaks of the experience of those who follow the Lord. That section concludes by stating that a righteous individual will be "like a tree planted by the rivers of water, that brings forth its fruit in season."[12]

There is nothing impractical or unrealistic in expecting trees or people to produce fruit in the right season. This is one point among several that makes a conversation Jesus had with a fig tree in the eleventh chapter of Mark remarkable.

Jesus was nearing the end of his earthly ministry when he walked up to this particular tree expecting to find some fruit. The problem was, Mark tells us, it was not the season for figs. Unfazed by the issue of the season, Mark tells us that Jesus spoke to the tree, saying, "Let no one eat fruit from you ever again."[13] The next morning as they passed by the same tree, they found it had completely withered.

By Jesus' actions we would conclude that He expected that the tree would produce fruit out of season as well as in. And if that is the case, what does He expect from of you and me?

In Matthew 25 we find the parable of the talents. In it Jesus tells of three servants who are entrusted with their master's goods as he prepares to depart for a lengthy journey. Two of the servants work diligently and produce twice as much as they had been given. The third servant buries what he had been entrusted with, and upon the master's return has nothing to show for what he had been given.

It is in the description of the character of the master that we learn something important. This third servant acknowledges, "Lord, I knew you to be a hard man, reaping where you have not sown, and gathering where you have not scattered seed. And I was afraid, and went and hid your talent in the ground."[14] The servant understood the master to be one who expected a return, even where he had not planted.

Similarly, your Master expects you to produce something pleasing in every situation, even those which arise because of the sin of others. The abusive treatment of Joseph by his brothers was not something that God willed these men to do. Nevertheless, God redeemed this situation to "save many people alive."[15] The enemies of the church were operating outside the will of God when they persecuted the early church.[16] Yet God purchased this situation to advance His purpose. The effect was that the dispersed church "went everywhere preaching the word."

It may not have been God who directly planted into your life the situations you are facing, but He does expect some measure of return from those situations.

In the story of the fig tree we learn this: the season is no excuse for fruitlessness because God wastes no season. He is working to bring about good in every situation. Jesus expects that in every season we will be producing good fruit.

Will you work with what you have been given and seek to produce something for God, or will you choose to bury the opportunity provided by your adverse situations?

Dangers in the Wilderness

* 9 *

THE film *Unbroken*, released in 2014, chronicles the story of Louie Zamperini, an American athlete who competed in the 1936 Berlin Olympics. Later he would join the U.S. Air Corps, and become a World War II bombardier in the South Pacific. On a routine mission Louie's plane crashed into the Pacific Ocean. There he would float with another surviving crew member for 47 days. The two men were eventually rescued by the Japanese navy, only to be interred at a series of prisoner of war camps where they experienced severe cruelty.

Louie's life did not initially seem that it would warrant a biography and major movie production. As a boy he often found himself in trouble with those in authority. In the biography of Louie written by Laura Hillenbrand, the descriptions of him as a boy ranged from "impish" to downright "dangerous."[1]

Despite the rough start, Louie's brother Pete saw potential in his younger brother as a long distance runner. Pete felt that if Louie could be recognized for doing something well, he may turn from his self-destructive route. Hillenbrand writes that Pete began forcing Louie to train every day as a track and field athlete. He would ride his bike behind his younger brother as he ran, "whacking him with a stick" to prod him to continue his training.[2]

During one particular scene early in the movie based on Hillenbrand's biographical work, Louie is ready to give up on his training. Pete responds by expressing his belief in his younger brother. Louie counters the confidence expressed by his brother, saying: "I don't believe." Louie would eventually respond to his brother's encouragement and accomplish what he thought was impossible.

I do not know what accomplishment you may achieve, but I do know that you will not achieve what you believe to be impossible. Proverbs 23:7 says, "As (a man) thinks in his heart, so is he." What you believe to be possible will go a long ways toward determining what will be possible.

As you recall, Jesus explained to Nicodemus, "The wind blows where it wishes…so is everyone who is born of the Spirit." Though the wind will blow where it wishes, that is not to suggest that it is beyond being hindered. We find in Louie's statement the first of two great dangers we face in the wilderness and the primary obstacle that will hinder the activity of God's Spirit within our lives, that being unbelief. We will not achieve what we believe to be impossible.

Remember earlier we noted that wherever Jesus went, the atmosphere was electric with possibilities. Everywhere, that is, except Nazareth. Here the atmospheric condition was skepticism. They did not believe that one like Jesus could ever arise from within their city limits because "nothing good ever came out of Nazareth."[3] All they had known was that which was unimpressive.

Unbelief was Nazareth's default setting. It prevented Jesus from doing anything substantial within their city limits. The same condition will attempt to rise up and threaten the work of God's Spirit within your life. Unbelief is a spiritual windbreak that will hinder the forward movement of the wind principle in your life. It rises up as a mountain which must be removed before progress can resume.

Notice again the cause of unbelief in Nazareth. They had never before known anything good to come out of their unimpressive city. They were bound by their experience. This was the same thing that hindered and threatened the movement of God within the life of Moses.

As God sought to call him out of the wilderness into his unexpected calling, it was a speech impediment that threatened to derail him along the route to his destination.[4] The only thing Moses had ever known was his struggle to speak. That being the case, how could he ever stand before Israel, much less Pharaoh, and command either authority or respect? Before he could ever leave the wilderness, this mountain would first have to be moved.

The Mountain of Unbelief

What is it that causes unbelief to impact the wind principle in such a significant way? We can answer that as we look back to Nazareth. It is not simply that Jesus decided that He would not perform any miracles there. More specifically, Mark says, "He could do no mighty work there."[5] Unbelief had the effect of tying God's hands.

In Psalm 78:41 we read much the same expressed as the Psalmist writes of ancient Israel: "Again and again they tempted God, and limited the Holy One of Israel."

As we look back to what happened when Israel first arrived at the border of the Promised Land in Numbers 13, we can identify a second effect of unbelief. Moses chose to send twelve men to spy out the land. Forty days later, when they returned, they reported that things were just as they had been told. "It truly flows with milk and honey," they explained. Despite the richness of the land, they concluded, "We are not able to go up against the people, for they are stronger than we."[6] Scripture explains that while exploring the land promised by God, the stature of the Canaanite inhabitants left them feeling as if they were little more than grasshoppers.

Despite the objections of Joshua and Caleb, two spies who returned with a faith-filled report, the damage had been done. The resolve of the people had been weakened; they were unwilling to move forward.

This is the second effect of unbelief. Not only does it tie God's hands, it also weakens ours. Your experience will never reach beyond what you believe to be possible. This generation of Israel never entered the Promised Land to take possession of it because they believed, with or without the help of God, that it was impossible.

In the Gospels we learn that Nazareth limited the mighty works of Jesus because all they had ever known was that nothing good came from Nazareth. This belief was a mountain which rose up based on what they had experienced. As long as this mountain was in the way, the residents of Nazareth would never experience anything special.

Mountains of unbelief can similarly rise out of our experience, effectively tying God's hands and weakening ours. "No one in my family has ever accomplished anything special." "I have always struggled in this area of life." These things can become mountains, and what we know of mountains is that they do not move.

In Matthew 21:21, we read of what Jesus has to say about the movability of mountains:

> "Assuredly, I say to you, if you have faith and do not doubt…if you say to this mountain, 'Be removed and be cast into the sea,' it will be done. And whatever things you ask in prayer, believing, you will receive."

Is it really possible to move a mountain? The answer depends on who you get as your mountain mover.

Dr. James Bradford is the General Secretary of the Assemblies of God. He holds a doctorate in aerospace engineering from the University of Minnesota. Dr. Bradford points out that in mathematics when you divide the number infinity by two, you get infinity. He says, "You cannot divide infinity into something smaller."[7] The point he is making is that God's ability never reaches a limit because His power is infinite. Because of this, it does not matter if the obstacle you face resembles a mountain or a molehill, God can move it.

I think it is time that we redefine mountains. That which stands in your way may be a mountain, but it is not immoveable. Your unimpressive beginning does not prevent God from taking you to an unexpectedly significant destination. Unhinge your future from your past. The only mountain that can hinder His work is the presence of unbelief.

We will never proceed beyond what we believe that God is able to do. At the same time, the mountain of unbelief is easily moved, simply by getting our eyes off the size of our obstacles and setting our focus on God who can do anything.

Practical Mountains

I would like to refer back to the account of Lazarus being raised from the dead. This man, a friend of Jesus and brother to Mary and Martha, had fallen ill. As his condition deteriorated, his sisters sent word to Jesus. By the time He arrived on the scene, Lazarus was already dead and had been in the grave for four days. We find the outcome of this in John 11:38-44. As you read the account, keep an eye out for something very obvious which had the potential of preventing a miraculous outcome:

"Then Jesus…groaning in Himself, came to the tomb. It was a cave, and a stone lay against it. Jesus said, 'Take away the stone.' Martha, the sister of him who was dead, said to Him, 'Lord, by this time there is a stench, for he has been dead four days.' Jesus said to her, 'Did I not say to you that if you would believe you would see the glory of God?'

"Then they took away the stone from the place where the dead man was lying. And Jesus lifted up His eyes and said, 'Father, I thank You that You have heard Me. And I know that You always hear Me, but because of the people who are standing by I said this, that they may believe that You sent Me.' Now when He had said these things, He cried with a loud voice, 'Lazarus, come forth!' And he who had died came out bound hand and foot with grave clothes…"

Did you find it, the practical thing that would have prevented the miracle? It was something easily handled, not requiring a command from Jesus or an act of God to address. It would not require faith to deal with, and yet dealing with it would require much faith.

If Lazarus was to come out of the grave alive, the rock would first need to be removed from the door of the tomb. Before the miracle would happen, the practical would have to be addressed. Just imagine if Jesus had called Lazarus back to life without first calling for the removal of the stone.

Although the practical could have been accomplished by any three or four strong individuals in the crowd, it still required a great deal of faith to accomplish. If I had been there, I suspect that I would have been thinking how uncomfortable things would become if Lazarus had not responded when Jesus called.

In nearly every situation there is something very practical which must happen before something miraculous will occur. In those instances, until the practical is done, the miraculous will not happen.

Late in 2014 I attended a ministry seminar in which I visited with a representative of Christians United for Israel who was present. After some initial introductions, he asked if I had ever visited Israel. I answered that I had not, but that it had long been my dream to do just that. He asked to pray with me that God would provide a way. I agreed and he proceeded to pray that God would go so far as to provide me with a free trip to the Holy Land.

After returning home, I wanted to pray in agreement that God would miraculously provide for me to go on such a trip. The problem was that there was a practical obstacle in the way that would prevent me from receiving the miracle, no matter how fervent my prayer. My passport was expired. Before I could ever receive the miraculous, I first would need to address that simple matter.

It may be that something like this was at the heart of Jesus' teaching about faith that moves mountains in Matthew 17:20. He explained that faith the size of a mustard seed was all that was needed to move a large obstacle.

It does not take much faith to update a passport, but without that level of faith, I would never experience the miracle. It does not take a lot of faith to fill out a job application or a mortgage application or to take an initial step of obedience, but without such practical steps, the miracle will always remain out of reach.

What would have happened if Jesus had raised Lazarus from the dead without commanding that the stone be removed? Poor Lazarus would have wandered around the inside of the cave waiting for death to take him a second time.

There is often a step we must take before the door will open to allow us to receive what is seemingly impossible. If we neglect the obvious things that stand between us and our desire, the miracle will die and we will miss it.

Watch Out for Ishmael

The second great threat we will face in the wilderness is, for lack of a better term, meddling. This danger arises because the wilderness often seems to be little more than a season of delay.

Perhaps this threat will manifest itself in your life in this way: You catch hold of the energizing truth that God has an exciting and unexpected destination that He is moving you toward. In response you unleash your heart and begin to believe for big things; you pray prayers of faith, you declare God's Word over your plans, and suddenly, nothing happens. For a long time. Years may pass. Even a decade or two. And so you start to meddle.

That is what happened with Abram and Sarai, later to be renamed Abraham and Sarah. In Genesis 12, God promised to make a great nation of Abraham, but there was a problem. He was seventy-five years old at the time and his wife was ten years his junior, and they had no children. At their age they had no reason to expect the stork to pay them a visit.

Ten years later they remained in the wilderness of literal barrenness when Sarah approached her husband with a plan: "See now, the Lord has restrained me from bearing children. Please, go in to my maid (Hagar); perhaps I shall obtain children by her."[8] We are told that Abraham listened to his wife and slept with her servant woman. Nine months later little Ishmael was born.

From the very beginning, their meddling in the plan of God brought contention to the household. Eventually Abram determined he had no choice but to send Hagar and Ishmael out on their own. As we read through the history of Israel in the Old Testament, we find that it was often the descendants of Ishmael who caused the greatest harm to the descendants of Abraham and Sarah.

Think back for a moment to Jesus' conversation with Nicodemus in John 3. There He explained: "That which is born of the flesh is flesh, and that which is born of the Spirit is spirit." When we meddle with God's plan, the result will always be flesh. In reality such interventions produce the opposite of the intended effect. The journey that would take us from the unimpressive beginning to the unexpected destination can be stalled, side-tracked or derailed altogether when we take matters into our own hands. We will never produce something spiritual by fleshly efforts.

Years later God explained that it would not be the son of the flesh through whom He would fulfill His promise to Abraham. Rather the fulfillment would come through another son, the son of the promise. Their meddling proved to be nothing more than a detour toward a dead-end.

During his own Wilderness University years, we see David with two prime opportunities to meddle in God's timing. In both instances David was presented with the opportunity to kill Saul and speed up his own ascension to the throne.[9] And why not?, he may have wondered. David had been chosen and Saul rejected. Why not help the process along and get Saul out of the picture? David's answer was that he had no right to harm the one God had chosen.

If we were to fast-forward several years, we would find David ill prepared to handle another opportunity to meddle. In 1 Samuel 29 we find the Philistines lining up, preparing to meet King Saul and Israel in battle. On the side of Israel's enemies we find an unlikely ally: David and his men. They are seemingly preparing themselves to join in battle *against* Israel. Perhaps things were simply moving too slowly for David, and he was now ready to meddle.

Imagine the damaging effect that this could have had on David's route from the sheepfold to the throne. It would ultimately be in this battle that Saul and his sons were killed. It was in this very conflict that the path to the throne was cleared for David.

Had David actually joined the Philistines in battle against King Saul, he could have been known as the traitor king rather than the shepherd king. After learning of Saul's death, those of the tribe of Judah quickly took steps to crown David as the new king. But how would they have responded had they known that David had fought on the side of Israel's most bitter enemy?

There are two things to take away from this story. First, David's meddling could potentially have derailed the route to the throne. It is doubtful that Judah would have rallied around a traitor king. Second and more relevant is that God sovereignly protected David from this outcome. David would have joined the Philistines in battle against Israel had they welcomed him. As it was, they feared that he may turn against them in battle, and they chose to send him and his men away.[10]

The flesh will always produce flesh. If David had fought against Saul alongside the Philistines, the result could have spelled disaster for David and all Israel. God mercifully prevented this outcome. He will do the same for you. At the same time, we must understand that if we persist in leaning on the flesh, God will allow us to taste the consequences.

In Ezekiel 14:4, God explains that because His people persisted in looking toward their idols, he would permit them to be deceived by their idols. The protection that they normally would have enjoyed would be removed because of their persistent rebellion.

The time spent in Wilderness University can seem like a complete waste. We feel that we should do something to move things along. And it is much more comfortable to do something than nothing. The fact is that God does have something for you to do now. He wants you to be faithful right where you are.

Think again of Moses, who worked as a shepherd while in the wilderness. In Exodus 3 we find that when God spoke to him out of the burning bush, Moses was tending sheep. He was being faithful where God had placed him. It will always be in faithfulness that the path out of the wilderness will be revealed.

My route in writing began, not with the goal of producing a book, but with the desire to create some ministry resources that would better serve our church. Writing grew out of my efforts to be faithful in the position in which I had been placed. Joseph's ascension to the position of second-in-command in Egypt came, not by seeking it out, but as he sought to be faithful and fruitful where he was, even though that place was prison.[11]

Wilderness Mirages

A mirage is an optical illusion with which we are all familiar. It results from the bending of light across a flat surface which will give the appearance of reality to something that is merely an illusion. We think we are seeing water down the road or across a barren wilderness, when in reality we are seeing a refracted image of the sky.

Mirages also exist in spiritual wildernesses.

Think again of Joseph in the book of Genesis. As a young man he became known as "the dreamer" after telling his family of his dreams that one day they would bow down to him. Motivated by envy, Joseph's brothers sold him into Egyptian slavery. Later he was falsely accused of assaulting the wife of his Egyptian master. I can imagine Joseph sitting in that Egyptian prison, wondering if the vision that God had placed upon his heart years earlier would ever come to pass.

One morning he awakened to learn that two fellow prisoners, Pharaoh's former butler and baker, were both troubled by dreams which they had dreamed the previous night. Joseph approaches the men saying, "Do not interpretations belong to God? Tell them to me, please."[12]

The men proceed to describe to Joseph what they had seen in their respective dreams. The interpretation of the dreams revealed that in three days the butler would be restored to his position of service to the king, while the baker in three days would be executed. As the butler walked out of the prison gates a free man, Joseph sent him out with this plea: "Remember me when it is well with you, and please show kindness to me; make mention of me to Pharaoh, and get me out of this house."[13]

I imagine that over the two or three weeks that followed, Joseph had a bit of a hop to his step. Every time he heard the prison doors rattle, he would expect that it was a messenger from the king bringing news of his release.

As weeks turned into a month, he began to entertain some doubts. What could be taking so long? Finally the cruel realization set in: he had been forgotten. The kindness he had shown to the butler had been returned with indifference. This experience was for Joseph a wilderness mirage. It was a situation which presented him with hope that his time in the wilderness would soon end. In the end, it proved to be nothing more than an illusion.

We can all relate to the way that Joseph must have felt, because we have all seen wilderness mirages. "Maybe this job application will get me out of the wilderness of unemployment." "Maybe this treatment will get me out of the wilderness of sickness." "Perhaps this will be the month of a positive pregnancy test and the end of the wilderness of barrenness." In Proverbs 13:12 we read this: "Hope deferred makes the heart sick." Every wilderness mirage will leave us feeling the same way.

In 2011 my wife and I celebrated Thanksgiving as we waited on the call that would lead us out of the wilderness of our daughter's year-long fight with liver disease. Two weeks prior to Malley's first birthday, we received the call for which we had been waiting. Her transplant coordinator called to tell us that an organ match had been found. We were told to leave for the hospital as soon as possible.

As we traveled, we knew that it was far from certain that our own wilderness experience was about to end. Just before taking the call from Minneapolis, we were in the emergency room in our hometown because of symptoms that suggested the presence of an abdominal infection caused by her failing liver.

Shortly after arriving at the hospital, our concerns were confirmed. The surgeon felt that the presence of the infection made the risk of surgery far too great. They would have to pass on the available organ. The hope brought by the phone call had been nothing but a mirage. It was an illusion that had left us grasping at something that was not to be, at least for that day.

In every wilderness there will be mirages. There will be times when what seemed like a certainty turns out to be an illusion. I can promise you there were times when Abraham and Sarah thought, "This is the month." For twenty-five years such hope proved to be nothing more than an illusion. Such times may well leave us feeling sick, thinking that it would have been better to have not hoped at all.

What we see in Abraham, and this is critical, is that the sick feeling brought on by deferred hope did not carry over to his faith. In Romans 4:18 we read that Abraham, "contrary to hope, in hope believed." Deferred hope will disappoint you, but it does not have to ruin you. As long as God is included in the equation, hope remains.

In the midst of twenty-five disappointing years and in spite of some meddling that added to his struggles, Abraham continued to believe. He did not allow his experience to that point to dictate his faith going forward. He did not tie God's hands or weaken his own through unbelief. The atmosphere surrounding Abraham's tent remained electric with possibility because they believed God. Oswald Chambers wrote, "Keep your life so constantly in touch with God that His surprising power can break through at any point. Live in a constant state of expectancy, and leave room for God to come in as He decides."[14]

At the front-end of Paul's second missionary journey, he arrived in the city of Philippi with his associate, Silas. Their experience to that point had been frustrating, but finally it seemed they were gaining some traction. That all changed when their ministry began to affect the pocket book of certain ones within the city. After a series of events, Paul and Silas were beaten and put in stocks within the jail in Philippi.

Luke tells us what followed as God worked to secure the release of His key ambassadors:

> "At midnight, Paul and Silas were praying and singing hymns to God, and the prisoners were listening to them. Suddenly there was a great earthquake, so that the foundations of the prison were shaken; and immediately all the doors were opened and everyone's chains were loosed" (Acts 16:25-26).

Suddenly always comes. There is always a time when the wilderness comes to an end. For Joseph *suddenly* arrived the day he was led into Pharaoh's throne room to interpret the king's troubling dreams. For Moses, it came as he turned aside to see the burning bush. For David *suddenly* came with the news that the path to the throne had been cleared.

The question is: when suddenly comes for you, will you still be waiting with expectancy, or will you have tied God's hands through unbelief? In Luke 18:8, Jesus questioned His listeners, saying, "When the Son of Man comes, will He really find faith on the earth?" When suddenly comes for you, will He find faith in you?

Section 3: An Unexpected Destination

Jerusalem, circa 998 B.C.

The king paused to catch his breath as he reached the small plateau on which stood the tent of meeting. Looking down the hill behind him he could see the roof of his palace where he had just spoken with the prophet Nathan. Turning back he stepped toward the tent.

This was not the original one constructed by Moses, but had been newly constructed by David's men as a place to house the Ark of the Covenant. The original tabernacle was at that time stationed at the high place in Gibeon where regular sacrifices were made to God. David had only recently called upon the Levites to bring the ark into the City of David.

He was a mix of emotions as he stepped toward his destination. Since the time of Moses, the house of the Lord had been a tent. It was embarrassing to the king to think that he lived in a house of cedar while the sacred ark dwelt in such a place. It had been his dream to build a permanent place for the worship of God within the walls of Jerusalem.

As he walked he looked farther uphill and to his left to the threshing floor of Araunah the Jebusite. It was there, on that platform that he had hoped to one day build a temple to his God. A cloud of chaff dispersed into the wind as the work of thrashing the grain continued. With it went his dream of seeing a temple built for God.

Turning back toward the tent, David climbed the final three stairs, finding himself on the platform on which stood the makeshift house of God. Several steps ahead stood a small altar on which the priests had just concluded the evening sacrifice. They were startled by the arrival of the king and discreetly excused themselves. Beyond the altar an equal number of steps hung the curtain which served as the doorway into the tent.

The king made his way around the altar until he was standing directly before the entryway. As a gentle breeze blew against his back, it caused the curtains to separate slightly, allowing him a momentary glimpse of what was housed within the Tent of Meeting. To the right stood a seven branch golden candlestick, a replica of the one constructed by Moses. The light it produced illuminated a breathtaking, albeit momentary, glimpse of the Ark of the Covenant.

David took the final few steps toward the entrance of the tent and entered. Cautiously advancing, he took a seat before the ark, his heart filled with reverent respect. He had learned a difficult lesson regarding that which God had set aside as sacred. His initial attempt to bring the ark to Jerusalem had ended in tragedy. On that occasion, David and his men had failed to transport it in the prescribed manner. This resulted in the death of one of his men, Uzzah, the son of Abinadab. The tragic incident taught him a somber lesson about properly handling that which was sacred.

David's visit to the house of God on this occasion was far different from any other. Generally his ascent would have been accompanied by the sights and sounds of music and worshipers. Today the king felt that silence and solitude would be the most appropriate expression of worship.

As he sat in silence, he considered the remarkable path that had taken him from the sheepfold to this unexpected place. He thought about the route that he had taken through the wilderness. It was a route that, to his shame, had led him to feign insanity before the king of the Philistines. It had also taken him from one cave to another in his flight from King Saul. Many times the route had left him asking, "What am I doing here?"

With the benefit of hindsight, he now fully realized that God had been directing his path the entire time. David's predecessor, King Saul, knew that David had been anointed to be his successor. In trying to secure the throne for one of his own sons, Saul had set out to kill David, in the process putting his own life at risk.

On two occasions Saul had inadvertently put himself in a position to be killed by David. In both instances, David had been encouraged by his men to take what God had rightly given him. "Kill Saul and take the throne," they had urged him.

But David was determined to avoid the mistakes Saul had made. He had heard first-hand from the prophet Samuel of Saul's first great error, taking on himself the responsibility of offering a sacrifice, a task reserved for Samuel alone. It was with that knowledge in hand that David determined he would never meddle with God's timing. The Lord would remove Saul from the throne when the time was right. David would have no part in such a somber task.

And then, unexpectedly, David received the news that Saul and his sons had been killed in battle. Though he understood that Saul would have to be dead before God's call on David's life would be realized, it was not a report that he relished.

He had never been afraid of displaying his emotions, but even he was surprised by the intensity of his grief. True, Jonathan had been closer to David than any friend or brother. For him, extreme grief was understandable. But as he wept on that day, David realized that his heart was broken, as much for Saul as for Jonathan. A short time later he would pen these words:

> "The beauty of Israel is slain on your high places! How the mighty have fallen! O daughters of Israel, weep over Saul. Jonathan was slain in your high places. How the mighty have fallen!"[1]

A shift in the wind caused David to catch a fresh scent of the incense from this simple house of worship, bringing him back to the moment. As unexpected as it was that God had chosen an unimpressive shepherd to shepherd the nation of Israel, equally so was that which God had spoken through the prophet Nathan concerning his future.

As he sat in silence, words of praise came to his lips, "Who am I, O Lord God? And what is my house, that You have brought me this far?"

David paused and thought again of the message God had given him through the prophet Nathan: "I took you from the sheepfold, from following the sheep, to be ruler over My people, over Israel." Every step along the route from the sheepfold to the throne had been as unexpected as it had been unpredictable.

David continued his impromptu praise chorus, barely above a whisper: "And yet this was a small thing in Your sight, O Lord God; and You have also spoken of Your servant's house for a great while to come. Is this the manner of man, O Lord God?"

During his years in the wilderness, David never doubted that the throne of Israel would be the destination of his life. After all, that is what God had called him to; and what could be beyond the throne? Now following his short conversation with the prophet Nathan, his vision was irrevocably set upon a new destination.

David now understood that God had a purpose and a plan for him that extended far beyond his own life. It was a plan that included his descendants for many generations to come. He recalled again God's words spoken through the prophet:

> "When your days are fulfilled and you rest with your fathers, I will set up your seed after you, who will come from your body, and I will establish his kingdom. He shall build a house for My name, and I will establish his kingdom forever."[2]

The destination was not what it had seemed. There was something beyond the throne that God had for David. God had set before the king a two-fold vision. His first task would be to prepare one of his sons to follow him as king over Israel. His second task would be to amass the materials necessary for constructing God's temple.

David wiped his face with his hands and took a moment to gather himself. He made a mental note that he would call a scribe as soon as he returned to the palace to capture the hymn of praise that had been on his heart as he had sat before the Lord. But now he stood, facing the sacred ark with a full heart. He had begun as an unimpressive shepherd, followed an unpredictable route through the wilderness to the throne, and now realized, unexpectedly, that the throne was not the destination. There was something ahead that God had for him. As he turned, exiting the tent, David took a step toward his palace and toward a future as unpredictable as it ever had been.

Defining the Destination

* 10 *

LET'S look again at the basis of the wind principle found in John 3:8. There Jesus, speaking to Nicodemus, says:

> "The wind blows where it wishes, and you hear the sound of it, but cannot tell where it comes from and where it goes. So is everyone born of the Spirit."

What we learn is that a degree of mystery always surrounds the operation of God's Spirit. We cannot predict the effect the wind will have upon that which it moves. Similarly we do not know the destination ahead as God's Spirit moves upon us. What we do know is that the movement of God in us is limited neither by our unimpressive beginnings nor by the raw material of our lives.

One of my favorite preachers and Bible teachers is Dan Betzer, pastor of First Assembly of God in Ft. Myers, FL. Listening to podcasts of his sermons, I have often heard him quote Hebrews 11:3, "By faith we understand that the worlds were framed by the word of God, so that the things which are seen were not made of things which are visible." Commenting on that, he has said, "If you feel like you have nothing, take heart! Nothing is the raw material that God used to create everything!" The point is you already possess everything God needs for creating something exciting.

There is another sense in which the destination is unknown.

We often hear of the importance of having a vision for life and having dreams and pursuing the plan of God. And rightly so, I would say. In Proverbs 29:18, we learn that without vision or revelation, people cast off restraint and perish.

But now, compare that with 1 Corinthians 2:9, a passage typically applied to the plan of God for His people in eternity:

"Eye has not seen, nor ear heard, nor have entered into the heart of man the things which God has prepared for those who love Him."

As I look at this passage in light of the wind principle, I believe that it clearly has something important to say about God's plans for you and me on this side of eternity. God has plans for us that cannot be predicted, at every stage of life. We have not begun to comprehend what He has in store. God's vision for your life is far beyond your vision.

It is the unpredictable nature of God's Spirit that makes this final aspect of the wind principle the most difficult to comment on. Generally when someone writes about a destination, they do so from the perspective of having already arrived there themselves. They tell of what it was like to reach the summit or win the gold or achieve their life's pursuits. There are many things I could write about from my personal experience, but reaching God's destination for my life is not one of them.

In Philippians 1:6, Paul says, "He who has begun a good work in you will complete it until the day of Jesus Christ." I do not know your eschatological beliefs, but I can confidently tell you that the day of Jesus Christ has not yet arrived. God's good work in your life is ongoing. You have not yet experienced the final chapter.

The Apostle Paul, in spite of all that he had accomplished for the kingdom of God, has concluded that even he had not yet reached his destination. "I press on," Paul writes, "that I may lay hold of that for which Christ Jesus has also laid hold of me. Brethren, I do not count myself to have apprehended; but one thing I do…I press toward the goal" (Philippians 3:12-13).

But what is the goal? What is the destination? That is what we need to define.

Growing up, our annual family vacation consisted of driving six hundred miles from our home in North Dakota to visit my grandparents in Nebraska. By most standards, it was an unimpressive vacation, but we loved every moment of it. Within the first few miles of our trip, one of us kids would teasingly ask my dad, "Are we there yet?"

One thing about the destination that is certain is that we know we have arrived once we get there. If you are still asking, "Am I there yet?" you can be certain that you are not.

Author and Christian apologist Ravi Zacharias has said, "The loneliest moment in life is when you have experienced that which was supposed to deliver the ultimate, and it has let you down." Many have reached what they figured would be the ultimate, the destination, only to find that they have been left yearning for something more. Unexpectedly, having reached the pinnacle, they find themselves disappointed by their lack of fulfillment.

Let's look again to King David and beyond to one of his descendants.

Four decades after David's death, his grandson Rehoboam became the king over Israel. He lacked both the spiritual commitment of his grandfather David and the wisdom of his father Solomon.

Of Rehoboam we read that shortly after being established as the king, "he forsook the law of the Lord, and all Israel along with him."[1] The result of his rebellion was that the nation quickly fell under the oppression of the Egyptians.

Later, when King Rehoboam and the nation reached out to God in humility, the Lord said, "They have humbled themselves; therefore I will not destroy them, but will grant them some deliverance...Nevertheless they will be his servants, that they may distinguish My service from the service of the kingdoms of the nations."[2]

God was determined to demonstrate to His people that serving the Lord was not as undesirable as they had come to believe, by allowing them to live under the rule of a foreign king for a time. So what is the difference between God's destination for your life or your own? How does serving God compare with serving yourself?

For starters, the pursuit of God's destination is the only pursuit that is undertaken without regret. In Proverbs 10:22 we read this: "The blessing of the Lord makes one rich, and He adds no sorrow with it." You will never find someone on a deathbed regretting the decision to spend life loving God or serving people. No one has ever stared death in the face regretting having spent too much time in God's Word or prayer. On the other hand, many have reached the end of their life regretting they had not given more thought to eternity or spent more time on their most important relationships.

Additionally, service to the Lord is the only place where there is the promise of something beyond the grave. Anything else you serve, be it pleasure, power, or wealth, both purpose and reward will die with you. The significance of this cannot be overstated. If you live for this world you are guaranteed to outlive your purpose.

Solomon speaks of this struggle when he writes, "I hated all my labor in which I had toiled under the sun, because I must leave it to the man who will come after me."[3]

Is it our lot to live out our lives pursuing the things we are supposed to pursue, only to find ourselves empty at the end and searching for more? God's Word answers, "No." There is a destination that will not disappoint. There is a purpose for your life that will outlast you.

As we seek to define the destination, there is a truth that emerges. It is simply this: You have not arrived. The Apostle Paul establishes this when he states that God will be faithful to continue his good work until the day of Jesus Christ. If we fail to understand this principle, we run the risk of falling short of the destination.

Is this a real risk? Paul believed so. In 1 Corinthians 9:27, he wrote, "I discipline my body and bring it into subjection, lest, when I have preached to others, I myself should become disqualified." He realized that he had not yet reached the destination, and that he always posed a risk to himself. The key point is that we must never view any pinnacle of success or achievement on this side of eternity as the ultimate destination.

One of the pivotal moments in King David's life is found in 2 Samuel 11. The chapter opens with these words:

> "It happened in the spring of the year, at the time when kings go out to battle, that David sent Joab and his servants with him, and all Israel; and they destroyed the people of Ammon and besieged Rabbah. But David remained at Jerusalem. Then it happened one evening that David arose from his bed and walked on the roof of the king's house. And from the roof he saw a woman bathing, and the woman was very beautiful to behold."[4]

The rest is, as they say, history. The woman he saw bathing was Bathsheba, the wife of Uriah, one David's most honorable soldiers. David had Bathsheba brought to him, slept with her, and after learning that she had become pregnant, conspired to have Uriah killed.

Let's travel back in the timeline of David's life from that point to an experience he had while enrolled in Wilderness University. We noted previously that on two occasions David had the opportunity to take Saul's life and claim the throne for himself. Though he had been anointed as Saul's successor, he refused to take something that was not his, the life of Saul. Compare those episodes to the matter of Uriah and Bathsheba, when he had no problem taking that which was not his.

On another occasion we find David and his men positioned outside David's hometown of Bethlehem, standing opposite the Philistine battle lines. As David looked down on the city and past the Philistine battle line, he became nostalgic, expressing his wish to have a drink from the well in Bethlehem.

The Bible tells us that three of his bravest men broke through the Philistine line for no other reason than to draw some water from the well to refresh David. The king was no doubt touched by their selfless act, but he refused to drink the water that had come to him at the risk of such a high price.

Borrowing a thought from author Ravi Zacharias, imagine how different Old Testament history would have been had David refused to drink the stolen waters that came to him in the form of Uriah's wife.[5]

Alongside the risk of disqualifying ourselves from the destination by some form of disobedience, there is another risk in prematurely believing that we have arrived.

Remember that Paul explained that it has not yet entered the mind of man, what God has in store for those who love Him. Regardless of where you are, God has something for you beyond where you are today. In Ephesians 3:20, Paul writes, "Now to Him who is able to do exceedingly abundantly *beyond* all that we ask or think, according to the power that works in us." God's plans and God's thoughts are beyond your present position.

When we prematurely believe that we have reached the destination, there is the distinct possibility that we may place constraints on what God can do. Think back to the way the people of Israel responded after sending spies into the Promised Land in

Numbers 13 and 14. Their faulty beliefs caused them to close their mind to the possibility that they could possess the land. An entire generation lost out because they believed that the border of the promise was the end of the route. They could not conceive of a scenario by which they would move beyond the border

Could it be today that what you perceive to be your destination might in reality be the border of the promise? Could it be that there is something beyond your present location that might help an entire generation move into what has been promised by God? Unhinge yourself from your own understanding and embrace the truth that what God has in His mind has not yet entered your mind. There is more beyond where you are today.

In Psalm 18:19, the psalmist writes, "He also brought me out into a broad place." God wants to move you to such a position. He wants to remove every self-imposed boundary and reposition your heart to believe for whatever destination God intends.

Eyes on the Unseen

We noted earlier that the pursuit of God's purposes is the only pursuit that is guaranteed to be without regret. The reason, in part, is that in every other pursuit both purpose and reward die with you. In serving the purposes of Christ, purpose and reward lie beyond the grave.

One of the most important things we can possess as followers of Christ is a vision of what lies beyond the grave. Without a vision of the eternal, it is highly possible that we will live for things that have no lasting value. Even for those who have followed Christ for years, there is a constant need to be urged to see beyond the here and now to the hereafter. The need to earn a living and the desire to excel, combined with the legitimate and illegitimate pleasure that is available, have the effect of constantly turning our focus to this side of eternity.

In 2 Corinthians 4:18, we read, "We do not look at the things which are seen, but at the things which are not seen. For the things which are seen are temporary, but the things which are not seen are eternal." We must be continually challenged to pursue eternal treasures rather than temporary treasures and to seek recognition in heaven above any that we might receive on earth.

The fact is, however, that we often only see the things that are visible with the natural eye. Many lack the vision to see the eternal. It was because of this that the great preacher Jonathan Edwards was said to have often prayed, "Lord, stamp eternity on my eyeballs."

Why is an eternal perspective so critical for you and me? Primarily because God's destination for us lies beyond the extent of our time here on earth. Again, we note the words of the Apostle Paul: "He who has begun a good work in you will complete it until the day of Jesus Christ."[6] That day should be the focus of our vision, because that is our destination.

So what will the day of Jesus Christ look like?

The Apostle John gives us the answer in his first epistle, where he writes:

"Beloved, we are the children of God; and it has not yet been revealed what we shall be, but we know that when He is revealed, we shall be like Him, for we shall see Him as He is."[7]

Notice that John says, "It has not yet been revealed." This hearkens back to the wind principle. We do not yet know exactly how or where the Spirit will move us, but what we do know is that our ultimate destination is beyond the scope of this life. What we live for is that moment when we stand before Jesus.

If anyone knew what it was like to stand before the glorified Christ, it was the Apostle John. He gives a commentary on his own eyewitness experience of that sight in the first chapter of the book of The Revelation. He writes of hearing a "loud voice, as of a trumpet" and seeing "One like the Son of Man." Describing the sight, he writes:

> "His head and hair were white like wool, as white as snow, and His eyes like flame of fire; His feet were like fine brass, as if refined in a furnace, and His voice as the sound of many waters; He had in His right hand seven stars, out of His mouth went a sharp two-edged sword, and His countenance was like the sun shining in its strength."[8]

What was the effect of this on the Apostle? In Revelation 1:17, he writes, "When I saw Him, I fell at His feet as dead."

No matter what you believe God has called you to or where you are currently positioned, this is what you are to live for: the moment when you stand face to face with Jesus.

What we can gather from John's description of his experience is that the encounter was indescribable. Everything paled in comparison to that moment. Similarly, every earthly destination we could pursue will pale when compared to the encounter that is to come.

God desires to get our vision off any destination on this side of eternity. Our focus should be affected by the realization that every one of us is destined for a face-to-face encounter with Jesus. A vision of eternity is what should define our destination.

Destined for Genuine Influence

AS we consider the route from the unimpressive beginnings to the unexpected destination, there are several assumptions that we often make. One of the first is that we expect our destination to be far from where we began. What we noticed, however, in looking at David is that though he moved from the sheepfold to the throne, he always remained a shepherd. He began in the sheepfold caring for sheep. He reached the throne where he was a shepherd of people.

We also tend to expect that the course of our life and influence will follow some type of a corporate ladder model. We expect that we will begin on the bottom rung as little more than a servant. From there, as we climb the ladder of influence, we assume the need to serve will decrease. As we reach the destination, we would ideally be at the height of influence with little need to be a servant.

Jesus addressed this tendency after the mother of James and John had asked that her sons be given the top two positions within the Lord's kingdom. Jesus responded:

> "You know that the rulers of the Gentiles lord it over them, and those who are great exercise authority over them. Yet it shall not be so among you; but whoever desires to become great among you, let him be your servant. And whoever desires to be first among you, let him be your slave—just as the Son of Man did not come to be served, but to serve, and to give His life a ransom for many."[1]

What we first need to understand about His instruction is that an insincere servant is no servant at all. I cannot operate with a mindset that I will become a servant in order to gain influence or authority. If that is the case I am only acting like a servant. The only way to be a real servant is to take on the mindset of a servant.

In Philippians 2:5-7, Paul urges us to take on the servant mindset of Jesus. He says:

> "Let this mind be in you which was also in Christ Jesus, who, being in the form of God, did not consider it robbery to be equal with God, but made Himself of no reputation, taking the form of a bondservant, and coming in the likeness of men."

There was no acting on Jesus' part. He did not act like a servant. He became a servant. Though He had real authority, He made Himself nothing.

Now consider, in the world system, what it is that gives people authority? Is it something inherent that individual possesses, or is it the position they hold that bestows the authority?

Take for example the President of the United States. The Commander in Chief may possess abilities that qualify that person to hold such a position of authority. But even then, it is not leadership qualities but the position that bestows the authority. That being the case, is there really anything particularly special about people with authority, considering that their only authority comes from their position?

Jesus taught and modeled a route to authority that does not require a position. The route is that of servanthood.

Now on the surface this may seem backward. But as we look deeper at the issue, who has more genuine authority: those whose authority is by virtue of their position or those who have gained authority without a position?

Once a servant, always a servant

We began this chapter by noting the tendency to believe that as influence increases, the need to be a servant decreases. Jesus countered that notion, explaining that servanthood is the preferred route to legitimate authority. The moment I begin to believe that my position exempts me from the need to serve is the moment that I move from real authority to that which depends upon my position.

A true leader understands that there is never a moment when the need to serve comes to an end. From the unimpressive beginning to the unexpected destination, your life should be marked by this conviction: "once a servant, always a servant." Serving is not a means to an end. It is the end. We do not serve because it is a route to a position of authority. We serve because it is the destination.

Although the call to be a servant never changes, the way we serve may.

Let's look at an example. In Acts 6:1-2, we find the leaders of the early church attempting to address a situation within the operation of the first church food pantry:

> "Now in those days, when the number of the disciples was multiplying, there arose a complaint against the Hebrews by the Hellenists, because their widows were neglected in the daily distribution. Then the twelve summoned the multitude of the disciples and said, 'It is not desirable that we should leave the word of God and serve tables.'"

Did these key leaders within the church view themselves as too high up to wait on tables? Certainly not, rather they saw that there was a call more critical than waiting tables that they were best equipped to answer, that being teaching and preaching.

A higher position might mean a different task, but it will never mean a different call. Your call is always that of a servant, and you will never rise beyond that call.

Jesus clearly illustrated His heart and the call to serve when He washed His disciples' feet; a task generally reserved for servants. At the close of that episode, He says:

> "You call Me Teacher and Lord, and you say well, for so I am. If I then, your Lord and Teacher, have washed your feet, you also ought to wash one another's feet. For I have given you an example, that you should do as I have done to you. Most assuredly, I say to you, a servant is not

greater than his master; nor is he who is sent greater than he who sent him. If you know these things, blessed are you if you do them."[2]

We will never be greater than our Master, and our Master was a servant. Once a servant, always a servant.

I think also that the timing of this episode is important to note. John reveals that it occurred during the Last Supper, the same evening on which Jesus would later be arrested. It would just be a few days after His entry into Jerusalem to cries of: "Hosanna! Blessed is He who comes in the name of the Lord! The King of Israel!"[3]

This was the height of His influence and the culmination of His ministry. Having reached His earthly destination, Jesus bowed down before each of His disciples and washed their feet. As He did, He explained, "A servant is not greater than his master."

By His timing He demonstrated that there was no point at which we will rise above the call to serve. "Once a servant, always a servant." Let His mind be in you.

Let's grab one last concept from the final phrase in this passage. Jesus concluded the thought saying, "Blessed are you if you do them." At times we may wonder how we will ever rise to a place of significance if we forever remain a servant. The answer to that is at the heart of the wind principle.

In his book, *Against the Flow*, John Lennox, Christian apologist and Oxford professor, points out something interesting from the call of Abraham in Genesis 12, where God says, "I will make your name great."[4] Lennox states that this comes on the heels of the story of the Tower of Babel in the previous chapter. He notes the vision of those building the tower: "Let us make a name for ourselves."[5]

There are two routes to reaching a place of significance in life. You can attempt to make a name for yourself, in which case you will be limited by your own abilities, by the opportunities which you come across, and by your ability to leverage them for your own advancement. Additionally, if you are going to make a name for yourself, you are going to have to fuel your own progress.

The other option is to leave the "name game" to God. Rather than living for the pursuit of significance, seek to position yourself to be moved by God's Spirit. What does He want to do with your life? One cannot know, but we do know that He can do anything He wishes with a life that is willing to go wherever the Spirit leads.

You don't have the energy to propel yourself toward the destination you have in mind, but the wind of God's Spirit will never tire. So get yourself in position to be moved.

How do we live in the here and now while living for the hereafter? By taking on the posture and heart of a servant. If you do, you will be blessed in what you do and end up right where God intends. And remember, the good that He has in mind for you has not yet entered your mind.

Insuring the Destination

* 12 *

I recall in high school basketball being teased by a classmate that regardless of how hard I worked, I would never be a professional basketball player. I can honestly say that I never dreamt that I would be in the NBA. I did dream of writing books.

The value of having dreams is not without support in the Bible. On the Day of Pentecost, when the "wind" of the Holy Spirit came upon those in the Upper Room, the Apostle Peter spoke up, explaining the event using the words of the Old Testament prophet Joel:

> "This is what was spoken by the prophet Joel: 'And it shall come to pass in the last days, says God, That I will pour out My Spirit on all flesh; your sons and your daughters shall prophesy, your young men shall see visions, your old men shall dream dreams.'"[1]

We see here then that dreams are directly tied to the activity of the Spirit in the lives of God's people.

Unfortunately, as empowering as dreams and vision can be, they can also have the effect of limiting the plans of God. Looking again at John 3:8, our key verse, we discover that there is always unpredictability to the activity of God's Spirit within the lives of God's people. Jesus explained that the work of God's Spirit is as unpredictable as the course of the wind. We have also noted that the good which God has in mind for you has not yet entered your mind.[2] God's best for you is better than what has entered your mind.

What is the point? By holding too tightly to our dreams, we may actually place constraints on what God would otherwise intend to accomplish.

Like a seed, the dreams and vision you have for your life are suggestive of what could be. If planted in the right soil and under good conditions, they may become a reality.

But this presents us with a challenge because before a seed can mature into a harvest, it must first be released from our hands. Harvest comes because in planting season, farmers choose to put their seed at risk by planting it in the ground. In placing their seed in the ground, they potentially expose it to loss by insects, flooding, drought or disease.

However, if they would have chosen to avoid the risk involved in planting the seed, they opened themselves to a guarantee of loss. Rodents, poor storage conditions or the passage of time would eventually ruin what they sought to save. Seed is saved, not by keeping it in storage, but by planting it in the ground.

What do you hope will be the produce of your life? In Mark 8:35, Jesus says, "Whoever desires to save his life will lose it, but whoever loses his life for My sake and the Gospel's will save it." It does feel risky to lose ourselves for the sake of the Lord. That is why we are so hesitant to give Him our lives without reservation.

One may question: "What if I don't like the direction in which God is moving me?"

While we may feel that there is too great a risk in surrendering control to God, Jesus explained that we guarantee loss by retaining control ourselves. Remember the farmer. He risks the loss of his seed by placing it in the ground, but guarantees the loss if he keeps it in storage.

Think for a moment of Abraham. At the age of seventy-five God promises him that a great nation would arise from his seed. Twenty-five years later, Isaac, the son of the promise, was born. Several years later in Genesis 22, God calls Abraham to place his only hope for the promise on the altar. There would be no second born son for Sarah. Isaac was the last and only hope. Yet without hesitation, Abraham set out, determined to obey God.

Abraham understood something critical. He knew that Isaac was safer on the altar of obedience than he would be remaining in the tent of disobedience. In Hebrews 11:19 we read that Abraham has concluded that "God was able to raise him up, even from the dead, from which he also received him in a figurative sense."

I think it all comes down to what we hope is produced through our lives. In speaking to Nicodemus, Jesus explained that the flesh always produces flesh. As long as I continue as the steward of my hopes and dreams, I will ensure that only flesh will be produced. On the other hand, if I place my hopes on the altar of surrender, inviting the Spirit of God into the equation, the return will be a guarantee of life and lasting fruit.

Who is the steward of your hopes and dreams? You may feel that you have the best in mind, and so you refuse to commit the process to God. The problem is that it does no good to retain stewardship if you lack the power to steward a hope into a reality. Even if you are convinced that your plan for your life is better than God's plan for your life, you have no ability to turn hope into reality.

The way to save what you hope for is not to hold onto it yourself. This ensures it will be lost. Rather, what we hope for must be entrusted to the stewardship of God. In giving it up, Jesus says that we will save it.

Death Precedes the Harvest

Shortly after entering Jerusalem on what we know as Palm Sunday, we find Jesus with his disciples teaching on the potential within a grain of seed. I can envision him walking over to a street vendor and picking a single grain of wheat from one of the baskets. Looking intently at that one kernel, He says:

> "The hour has come that the Son of Man should be glorified. Most assuredly, I say to you, unless a grain of wheat falls into the ground and dies, it remains alone; but if it dies, it produces much grain. He who loves his life will lose it, and he who hates his life in this world will keep it for eternal life."[3]

The vision and dreams you hold for your life are no different. Their potential is limited as long as they remain within your control.

Let's return one final time to the parable of the talents in Matthew 25:14-30. The setting of this parable, you will remember, is a master leaving for a long trip and entrusting his resources into the hands of three servants. The first two servants were faithful with the resources delivered into their hands, and they earned back twice as much for their master.

When the third servant is called to account, he says, "Lord, I knew you to be a hard man, reaping where you have not sown, and gathering where you have not scattered seed. And I was afraid, and went and hid your talent in the ground. Look, there you have what is yours."[4]

To help develop this thought, we also need to note the creation of man in Genesis 2:7, where we read, "The Lord God formed man of the dust of the ground, and breathed into his nostrils the breath of life; and man became a living being." You and I are made of the same "ground" in which the worthless servant buried his talent.

Let's bring this together now.

Why is it that we are hesitant to commit our dreams and vision to God? Is it not because we are afraid? We either fear that God will not give us back what we have committed to Him, or we fear what He will expect of us. So we determine to retain control. We keep those dreams close to our heart. In a sense, we bury them in our flesh, the dust of the earth.

The problem with this is, as Jesus told Nicodemus in John 3:6, that flesh can only give birth to flesh. By its nature it can produce nothing else.

Since you are reading this book, I suspect that you desire to see God accomplish something significant with your life. You do not want your harvest to be that which is produced by the flesh, rather you want what can be produced when the Spirit of God has free reign to move in your life. You want to see where the Wind of God's Spirit will move you.

If that is the case, you must get out of the flesh and into the Spirit. Your dreams and vision must be released from your hand and committed to God's care. In a sense, they must first die to you so that a harvest from God can be received.

Will God give you back what you have entrusted to Him? It is impossible to predict the specifics of what He will do. Remember, no one can predict the wind. But what we can predict is that it will be beyond what we have imagined.

To understand what God will do with what we have placed into His hand, it is essential that we understand His nature. In Psalm 107:1 we discover that God is good. Goodness is part of His nature.

Now we move to 2 Timothy 2:13 where we read, "(God) cannot deny Himself." This means that God will never act in a way that is contrary to His nature. He will always be good, which means that the destination of His work in your life will be good.

You can ensure the good destination today by releasing the seed from your hand into God's hand. Allow your dreams to be buried in His purposes, and open your heart and mind to more than you can ask or think.

Divine Goodness & An Unexpected Destination

* 13 *

AT this point we must address a challenge that will inevitably arise within as we consider trusting God to lead us toward our unexpected destination. The challenge may come in the form of a question: Will I like where God leads me?

If you grew up in the Church, you may have worried about giving your life completely to Jesus. What if He calls me to be a missionary in some undesirable location? Or as a young adult you may have feared: What if I am called to be single my entire life? Or think about this frightening scenario: What if I am called to be a single missionary in some undesirable location?

Seriously though, at the heart of the matter is found what I believe is our greatest challenge in relating to God; the struggle to trust that God is good. We seem to have little problem believing that God is just or loving or even all-powerful. But for some reason, we find it extremely difficult to believe that He is always good. Why is that?

I think the answer is simple enough. Our experiences are not always good. And since our experiences are not always good, we begin to question, can God be good? After all, isn't it logical to conclude that a good God will keep me from bad experiences?

To correctly answer these all-important questions, it is essential that we accurately define what really constitutes goodness. The fact is that goodness is not an objective reality. Every one of us judges what is good by the perspective of our life experiences.

Take as an example the discipline of a child. When a parent disciplines a child, the parent is in fact, displaying goodness; though from the perspective of the child, the correction is not good. The child would most likely define that discipline as bad.

Now consider the way you perceive the discipline you received as a child, assuming you received any. If your parents lovingly corrected you, it is almost certain that you now perceive the discipline you received as a good thing.

In this first simple instance, we find that the definition of goodness is based entirely on the perspective of one's experience.

Take as another example the sentencing of a convicted criminal by a judge. When a judge sentences a violator in accordance with the law, he is displaying goodness. He is being a good judge, but from the point of view of the criminal, there is nothing good about what the judge has done.

So to correctly perceive God's goodness, we must first be able to see things from His perspective. If we do not, we will always be wrong in our perception of His goodness.

There is an additional important truth we discovered in these two examples. It is this, that goodness will not necessarily be manifested by good experiences. If God's goodness flows out of a perspective entirely different from my own, it is quite possible that God is manifesting His goodness in the midst of experiences that are not good. To even begin to accurately judge the goodness of God, I must first be able to see things the way He sees them.

Before we can even begin to judge His goodness, we must first answer this question: Is God's perspective and my perspective the same? Before we settle on what seems to be an obvious answer, let's look more closely at the question. I believe that what we find will prove extremely important.

Perspective #1 – God's Understanding

The knowledge of God seems like a logical place to start as we seek to understand the perspective out of which He operates. Let's begin with some insight from the Apostle Paul out of the book of Romans:

> "Oh, the depth of the riches both of the wisdom and knowledge of God! How unsearchable are His judgments and His ways past finding out."[1]

What Paul is expressing is that if God's understanding were a gold mine, it would be impossible to fully draw out the entirety of His wisdom and knowledge.

The Lord Himself helps us further understand the disparity between our knowledge and His, when He says, through the prophet Isaiah:

> "My thoughts are not your thoughts, nor are your ways My ways…For as the heavens are higher than the earth, so are My ways higher than your ways, and My thoughts than your thoughts."[2]

The Bible reveals that the Lord God operates at a level far beyond our own capacity to understand. If you are in a place in which you feel that you cannot understand what God is up to, take heart, the Bible reveals that you are experiencing precisely what you should expect to experience.

At this point someone will inevitably argue: "That is a cop-out. You cannot dismiss bad experiences by suggesting: God is still good, we are just unable to grasp His understanding."

While I understand that point, it is critical to realize that this is simply what Scripture reveals. The God of the Bible has understanding that vastly exceeds man's. Scripture reveals that you cannot judge God's goodness, or lack thereof, based on your experience because you cannot possibly comprehend the perspective from which He is operating.

The story has been told of a believer who once spoke to an atheist, suggesting, "Why don't you tell me about the God you don't believe in. Maybe I don't believe in Him either." The point the believer was making was that perhaps the "god" the atheist rejected was really no god at all.

The fact is that the Bible does not present a god with the same level of understanding as man. The God revealed by the Bible is One with understanding far superior to our own. So if you want to make a judgment about God's goodness, make sure that your assumptions of God are correct.

What are the implications of this first point? We have already demonstrated that the perception of goodness is entirely subjective. So unless we can view things from God's perspective, we literally have no ability to accurately judge His goodness.

Perspective #2 – God's Eternal Point of View

There is a second perspective from which God operates, and it too is far different from our own. It is the perspective of time.

In Revelations 1:8, Jesus communicates to the Apostle John, "I am the Alpha and Omega, the Beginning and the End." The Bible reveals that God is able to see the beginning, the present and the end. It is out of this perspective that He operates. Everything He does flows out of His full knowledge of the span of time. He knows what every experience will produce.

Now let's compare God's comprehension of time with our own. You have probably heard the saying, "Hindsight is 20/20." It means that when we look back on our lives, we can more clearly perceive what it was that actually happened. This is why some say, "If I could have only known then what I know now." The past is the first dimension of time which we have the capacity to accurately perceive.

The second dimension of time which we are able to view well is the present. We may not know why something is happening or what the result will be, but we know that it is. As I am writing this sentence, I don't know if anyone will want to read it, but I do know that I am writing it.

It is here that our capacity to see comes to an end. Like a wise man once said, "As far as seeing into the future, we can't see beyond the end of our nose."[3] I have no idea what will come tomorrow. As I write, I know that tomorrow will be a Friday and I know what I plan to do, but I do not have any idea of what may actually transpire.

The point of all this is to again demonstrate that God operates from a perspective far different from our own. I am limited in my vision. God is not. I can see the past and the present. God can see the past, present and the future. Again, I cannot accurately judge the goodness of God because I cannot see things from His perspective.

The English poet, William Blake, has written:

> This life's dim windows of the soul
> Distorts the heavens from pole to pole
> And leads you to believe a lie
> When you see with, not through, the eye.[4]

What Blake is pointing out is that our limited vision threatens to continually distort our perception. If my senses alone are what inform my understanding of God's goodness, I will certainly come to an erroneous conclusion about His activity in my life.

The scope of God's vision is far greater than my own. Before I will ever understand His activity in my life, I must first see as He sees.

Any experience-based judgments we make about the goodness of God are almost certainly wrong because they are based on a faulty assumption. That assumption is the belief that I can judge in the present moment what God knows from beginning to end.

How is all of this relevant to our subject?

The wind principle states that God will move us from our unimpressive beginnings toward an unexpected destination. We stated that the destination that God is moving a believer toward will always be in line with His nature. The Bible reveals that God is good. That means the destination of His activity in our lives will likewise be good.

The problem is, if we struggle to believe that God is good, it will be extremely difficult for us to entrust our future to His care. And if we are unwilling to commit our future to Him, we will never reach the destination that He intends for this life on earth.

When we begin to grasp an accurate understanding of divine goodness, we find that really bad experiences should not cause us to call into question the goodness of God. His goodness operates from a perspective we do not possess. He is good, He knows more than we do, and He sees what we cannot see. Regardless of your bad experiences, you can trust Him to take you from where you are to a good destination.

The Daily Destination

* 14 *

THROUGHOUT the course of this book, we have discovered that God intends to move His people from their unimpressive beginnings along an unpredictable route toward an unexpected destination. The struggle, of course, is to remain on course when we do not know the specifics of where we are going or how we are going to get there. To a degree, we can associate with the sentiments of Thomas when Jesus told the disciples, "Where I go you know, and the way you know." To that, Thomas responded, "Lord, we do not know where You are going, and how can we know the way?"[1]

We could say something similar. "Lord, we do not know where *we* are going; how can we know the way?"

That is the type of question Abraham may have felt like asking when he was called to leave his home and family and settle in an undisclosed location.[2] God effectively told him that he would know where he was going once he arrived. I'm not sure that would be terribly comforting. To me it sounds similar to what God told Moses in Exodus 3:12, when Moses sought some assurances from

God. The Lord responded, "This shall be a sign to you that I have sent you: When you have brought the people out of Egypt, you shall serve God on this mountain."

Comforting or not, this is what the walk of faith is all about. There must come a time when we determine that we will trust that God will lead us to a good destination. Like Abraham, we must determine that we will go out though we may be uncertain where we are going.[3]

As we look more closely at Abraham, we find an important truth, which is this: our final destination will be determined by our daily decisions. Abraham ultimately reached his destination because when God called him to go, he went. Along the way there were many additional daily decisions that kept him on track or resulted in him being temporarily sidetracked.

In Galatians 6:7 we find this spiritual law: "Do not be deceived, God is not mocked; for whatever a man sows, that he will also reap." Our present location is the product of past decisions, and our present decisions will go a long way toward determining our future destination.

While maintaining our focus on the final destination, we must always keep an eye on our present location. Because, as Andy Stanley states in his book, *The Principle of the Path*, "Direction, not intention, determines destination."[4]

This may cause you to call into question a central element of the wind principle. Previously, we stated that the final destination could not be predicted by our current location. Now we are suggesting that the final destination is determined by today's decisions.

The answer to the apparent contradiction may lie in the difference between location and position. God was able to move David from the sheepfold, through the wilderness and to the throne, not because David was in the right place at the right time (location) but because his heart remained in the right place (position).

Though his location, the sheepfold, said nothing of his ultimate destination, the position of his heart did. In this sense, David remained in a position that would allow him to be moved by God.

We need to begin to view the destination, not so much as a position of influence or a place of success, but rather as a daily place where we are able to be led by God. The destination does not depend so much on you being in the right place at the right time, as it does on your heart being positioned in the right place.

There are many things about the Spirit's desired destination for us that lies beyond our ability to control. There is one thing, however, that is entirely within our control, and that is the position of our heart. We can control whether or not we place limits on God through unbelief. It is our choice to either meddle with the process or entrust it to God. We have the capacity to choose if we will believe that God's goodness is greater than our own. Every position of the heart is within our control and will be predictive of our future destination.

There are important lessons we can learn by looking at Abraham's journey from his home in Ur to a then unknown destination. In Hebrews 11:9-10, we read, "By faith (Abraham) dwelt in the land of promise as in a foreign country, dwelling in tents…for he waited for the city which has foundations, whose builder and maker is God."

At this point I'd like to highlight a point that has been previously made, that being the importance of understanding that the ultimate destination lies beyond the scope of this life. Although Abraham had reached the land of promise, he continued to live as a foreigner, keeping his focus on an eternal destination.

Finally, from the life of Abraham, we find an additional lesson found in a short description of Abraham's accommodations. We are told that his years in the land of promise were spent "dwelling in tents." He never put down roots.

Abraham lived ready to move. If God ever came to him and said it was time to resettle elsewhere, it would only require the pulling of a few tent stakes and he would be ready to go.

Are we so positioned that we are ready to be moved when and where the Spirit sends us? Remember, reaching the destination that God has in mind is not dependent on you being in the right place at the right time. What it does depend on is you having a heart that is in the right position when the time is right.

Seek to uproot any mindset that finds its origin in your personal history or your present position. Such mindsets will potentially place constraints on the activity of God within your life. Embrace the truth that just as the wind blows wherever it wishes, so God's Spirit can move you wherever He wishes. Make it your goal to live every day in such a way that you can be moved by God's Spirit.

Acknowledgements

I would like to begin by expressing thanks to my wife, Jennifer, for her loving care of our family, and for all that she adds to the ministry efforts within our church.

Thank you to my church in Valley City. I am grateful for the opportunity you provided me when I joined you years ago. Thank you for the manageable expectations you placed on me which allowed me the opportunity to grow. Thanks also for giving me space to work on these extra projects and for allowing me to run much of this material past you first.

Thanks to my proofreaders and editors: Vicki Jackson, my dad, Leroy Aufenkamp, Mr. Warren Schlecht and Hannah Dockter. Your work on the project was invaluable.

Thanks to my mentor in ministry, Bob Knight. Your investment in my life has been an incredible blessing to me.

Thanks also to my mother, Bev and my siblings, Lindsey, Matthew and Nathan for always being an encouragement to me.

Endnotes

Chapter 1 – A Long Shot

[1] Metaxas, Eric. *Seven Men: And the Secret of Their Greatness.* Nashville: Thomas Nelson, 2013, 58.
[2] Psalm 139:16

Chapter 2 – Lynchpin

[1] Matthew 22:17
[2] John 8:1-11

Chapter 3 – Out of the Sheepfold

[1] John 1:46
[2] Jesús, Wilfredo De. *Amazing Faith: How to Make God Take Notice.* Springfield, MO: Influence Resources, 2012, ebook.
[3] 2 Samuel 7:8-9
[4] Luke 3:2
[5] Jeremiah 1:6
[6] 1 Samuel 17:47

Chapter 4 – The Secret Place

[1] James 1:6-7
[2] Acts 8:4
[3] Acts 12:5

Chapter 5 – The Fuel

[1] John 16:13
[2] Zacharias, Ravi K., and Normal L. Geisler. *Who Made God?: And Answers to over 100 Other Tough Questions of Faith.* Grand Rapids, MI: Zondervan, 2003, 65.
[3] See Phillip E. Johnson, *The Wedge of Truth.* Downers Grove, IL: InverVarsity, 2000, 153.
[4] See Ravi Zacharias, *Can Man Live Without God.* Dallas: Word Publishing, 1994, 18.

---

[5] For a fascinating perspective on the days of creation, I recommend *Seven Days that Divide the World* by John Lennox.
[6] 2 Kings 6:8-23

Chapter 6 – Giants Moments

[1] Houghton, Frank. *Amy Carmichael of Dohnavur*. London: S.P.C.K., 1953.
[2] 1 Samuel 10:9
[3] 1 Samuel 16:7
[4] 2 Chronicles 16:9
[5] 1 Samuel 16:12
[6] Exodus 13:18
[7] 1 Samuel 17:36
[8] 1 Samuel 17:29
[9] Acts 20:22-23
[10] Acts 21:10-11
[11] Xenophon. *Anabasis.* Book 3.3.2.
[12] Xenophon. *Anabasis:* Book 3.3.4.
[13] Judges 20:16
[14] 1 Chronicles 12:1-2
[15] 1 Samuel 17:48
[16] 1 Samuel 17:46-47
[17] King James Version
[18] Hebrews 11:34, 36
[19] Jeremiah 43:4-7
[20] Revelation 1:18
[21] Zacharias, Ravi K., and Vince Vitale. *Why Suffering?: Finding Meaning and Comfort When Life Doesn't Make Sense.* New York: FaithWords, 2014, 80
[22] Zacharias and Vitale, 203-204
[23] See 1 Peter 1:18-19

Chapter 7 – Wilderness University

[1] 1 Samuel 21:10
[2] Redpath, Alan. The Making of a Man: Studies in the Life of David. Westwood, NJ: Revell, 1962, 67.
[3] Hebrews 5:2
[4] 1 Peter 4:12-13
[5] Luke 22:42
[6] Matthew 27:46
[7] Luke 23:41
[8] Mark 4:38
[9] Matthew 27:46

[10] Job 2:9
[11] Zacharias, Ravi. *Can Man Live Without God?*. Nashville, TN: W Pub. Group, 1994, 186.
[12] Ibid.

Chapter 8 – *God's Will in the Wilderness*

[1] 1 Thessalonians 5:18
[2] Matthew 26:39
[3] Matthew 26:26-27
[4] Genesis 25:31
[5] Genesis 25:34
[6] 1 Timothy 6:6
[7] Luke 17:14-16
[8] Luke 17:19
[9] Ecclesiastes 11:5-6
[10] Isaiah 32:20
[11] Ecclesiastes 11:4
[12] Psalm 1:3
[13] Mark 11:14
[14] Matthew 25:24-25
[15] Genesis 50:20
[16] Acts 8:1

Chapter 9 – *Dangers in the Wilderness*

[1] Hillenbrand, Laura. Unbroken: A World War II Story of Survival, Resilience and Redemption. New York: Random House, 2014, 11.
[2] Hillenbrand, 15
[3] John 1:46
[4] Exodus 4:10
[5] Mark 6:5-6
[6] Numbers 13:31
[7] Bradford, James. *2 Chronicles 7:14: A 28-Day Journey in Prayer*. 1st ed. Springfield, MO: My Healthy Church, 2013, eBook.
[8] Genesis 16:2
[9] See 1 Samuel 24:1-22 and 26:1-25
[10] See 1 Samuel 29:11
[11] See Genesis 39:20-23
[12] Genesis 40:8
[13] Genesis 40:14
[14] Chambers, Oswald. *My Utmost for His Highest*. New York: Dodd, Mead & Company, 1956, 25.

Introduction, Section 3: The Unexpected Destination

[1] 2 Samuel 1:19,24,25,27
[2] 2 Samuel 7:12-13

Chapter 10 – Defining the Destination

[1] 2 Chronicles 12:1
[2] 2 Chronicles 12:7-8
[3] Ecclesiastes 2:18
[4] 2 Samuel 11:1-2
[5] Zacharias, Ravi. *I, Isaac, take Thee Rebekah.* Nashville, TN: W Pub. Group, 2004, 75.
[6] Philippians 1:6
[7] 1 John 3:2
[8] Revelation 1:10,13-16

Chapter 11 – Destined for Genuine Influence

[1] Matthew 20:25-28
[2] John 13:13-17
[3] John 12:13
[4] Genesis 12:2
[5] Genesis 11:4

Chapter 12 – Insuring the Destination

[1] Acts 2:16–17
[2] See 1 Corinthians 2:9 & Ephesians 3:20
[3] John 12:23-26. Some will criticize Jesus' illustration, arguing that a seed does not die when planted in the ground. It is important to note, however, that the seed of which He spoke was His body, and not a literal grain of wheat. This statement is similar in form to what He said in John 2:19: "Destroy this temple, and in three days I will raise it up." In answering critics of this preposterous notion, John explained that the temple of which He spoke was His body (vs. 21).
[4] Matthew 25:24-25

Chapter 13 – Divine Goodness and the Unexpected Destination

[1] Romans 11:33
[2] Isaiah 55:8-9
[3] Most recently from The Reverend Leroy Aufenkamp
[4] Blake, William. *The Everlasting Gospel.* Bandanna Books, 2011, 19.

Chapter 14 – The Daily Destination

[1] John 14:5-6
[2] See Genesis 12:1
[3] See Hebrews 11:8
[4] Stanley, Andy. *The Principle of the Path: How to Get from Where You Are to Where You Want to Be.* Nashville, TN: Thomas Nelson, 2008, 95.